NEW
Marriage,
SAME
Couple

DON'T LET YOUR WORST
DAYS BE YOUR LAST DAYS

JOSH AND KATIE WALTERS

W PUBLISHING GROUP

AN IMPRINT OF THOMAS NELSON

This book is dedicated to you, the reader.

NOTE TO THE READER

I'm not sure what season of marriage you find yourself in; however, by picking up this book you've expressed the desire to have a new marriage. Before getting started be assured, it can be yours! Whether you are in a moment of crisis and hope seems lost. Or, if you are happily married but aware of the need to grow in your relationship and get to a new place. That desire coupled with this book and workbook will help you experience immeasurably more than you could ask or imagine in the one relationship that matters most! If that was in any way dependent on Katie and I, it would be an audacious claim. But we believe it to be the heart of God, and with Him anything is possible. He does not want you to have a miserable, mediocre, or mundane marriage. Do you believe that? Ultimately, this is a work only He can do. But only you can read the book and put in the work.

John 10:10 says, "The thief's purpose is to steal and kill and destroy. My purpose is to give them a rich and satisfying life." I'm not sure how you would describe your current experience in marriage. But if you are looking for "rich and satisfying," get ready—it's coming for you! We can't wait to see what God does in your marriage.

CONTENTS

CONTENTS

W hat if it's me?" Katie asked.

One of her best friends had just left the house. It wasn't unusual for this neighbor to come over to our house for a chat with Katie, but it was one of the few times I (Josh) had been pulled into the conversation. She told us she had been struggling in her marriage, that something didn't feel right. She said her husband seemed absent—distant physically and unengaged emotionally. She was hurting, and they were in a tough spot.

We'd listened to her concerns, encouraged her, and prayed

together. She was afraid there was someone else. I confidently told her, "There's no way." I knew her husband. He wouldn't do that. After she left, Katie and I remained sitting in the kitchen, mostly in silence.

As I tried to process everything our friend had just told us, I was reminded that our marriage also had not been easy. I thought our struggles had been normal, though. We were in a season of life where we'd started having children, were getting our master's degrees, were working full-time, and had acquired a few rental properties. There was a lot going on, and figuring out how to build the marriage of our dreams wasn't coming easy. There had been lots of arguments, frustration, and disappointments. But there was also a fair amount of sex, date nights, and Jesus. I thought we were moving in the right direction.

Katie's question didn't make sense to me. I was not connecting the dots. "What are you talking about?"

Seeing her anxiety, my confusion turned to anger as the gears finally began to turn. "What are you saying?" I yelled. I stood up and started walking toward the front door. We were not talking about some guy from work or a stranger she had met somewhere (not that it would have been easier). He was one of my best friends. I thought, *If she's saying what I think she's saying, I'm going over there right now!*

A few minutes later, the four of us were in the front yard screaming and crying, broken. "What have you done? How could you do this to me?" I cried.

Much of that night is a blur, but in the coming months I

started to see things in high definition as I learned about all the phone calls, letters, gifts, time spent, and things they'd done together. There had been a lot of time devoted to pursuing, responding, and daydreaming about a relationship outside their marriages. But that night, I was devastated to learn that the "someone else" our friend had been afraid of . . . was my wife.

Katie's question that night cracked open the door to what was going on between her and the other man. But it also served as an invitation to reality—a wake-up call to the fact that things were not as they seemed in our relationship. I'd seen marriages fall apart. We'd walked with couples who had drifted apart over a number of years, some who'd been unfaithful with others—but certainly that would never happen to us. We were different.

FOR BETTER OR FOR WORSE

Have you ever thought that your marriage is bulletproof? That nothing serious could come between you and your spouse—certainly not an affair? Maybe your confidence is rooted in your love for God; in the example modeled by your parents or grandparents; in the convictions you hold, the vows you made, the number of years you've been together, the shared dream of growing old together; or in your general optimism and positivity.

John 10:10 has always been an anchor verse for us: "The

thief comes only to steal and kill and destroy. I came that they may have life and have it abundantly" (ESV). We etched it in driveways, hung it in our home, and pursued that promise in our marriage. Abundant life! Don't you want some of that? It's available for all of us. But we (and maybe you as well) had been living as if the first part of that verse were not true. We have an enemy who is seeking to destroy what God has called good. Marriage is a gift from God. He said, "It is not good for the man to be alone. I will make a helper suitable for him" (Gen. 2:18). Through this relationship we experience and model to the world God's covenant love for us. That He will never leave us or forsake us (Heb. 13:5).

For better or for worse, for richer or for poorer, in sickness and in health. We say those words and mean them. Until we don't. It turns out, given the right circumstances, none of us are exempt from drifting apart or making bad decisions that lead us to places we never thought we'd go. For you, what you're experiencing may not be the betrayal of an affair. We pray it's not. But perhaps you're not experiencing the abundant life you'd always dreamed of with your spouse.

This is a book about what to do when you find yourself there.

S.T.A.Y.

If we are honest with ourselves, we tend to avoid physical or emotional pain. We often start looking around for a new job when things get hard at work, when the new boss is a jerk, or when we're tired of doing the same thing every day. Professionally, deciding to leave and pursue something new can work out in our favor. Maybe we'll find a better work environment, a boss we enjoy, and start making a little more money. But what do you do when you feel that way in your marriage? When things are hard, your spouse acts like a jerk, and you're tired of the same things every day? It's very common in our culture to see couples take the same approach they would in their careers—look for something better.

Pain is an indicator that something is wrong. That something needs to be done. Instead of your leaving, checking out, or looking elsewhere to be satisfied, what if God wants to use the pain you are feeling to help you build a new marriage . . . with the same person? That is our story. God did that in our marriage, and we are confident He can do it in yours.

Getting there is a process. This book lays out the principles we learned in that season when God healed and restored our marriage. This process is broken into four parts and is an acronym for the word S.T.A.Y.

Start with me.
Take quitting off the table.
Allow others to be part of the story.
Yield to vision.

Each of these steps is unpacked in the four parts of this book. We believe you want to stay; I think that's why you picked up this book. Most importantly, I believe it's what God wants for you.

We're not talking about getting back to an old place, to a

love that you once shared or an attraction you once had. We're talking about going to a new place. A deeper place. You can experience the marriage you've always wanted.

Keep reading and know that Katie and I are praying for you, believing your best days are ahead!

Part One

START WITH ME
TAKE QUITTING OFF THE TABLE
ALLOW OTHERS TO BE A PART OF THE STORY
YIELD TO VISION

When your marriage feels broken or when things get tough, it's easy to look at all the faults in the other person. You may even feel hopeless, wondering if things could ever change between the two of you. But the first step, perhaps the hardest one, in healing or strengthening a marriage is to look at your contributions to the problem. It takes courage and faith, but I know you are up for it because you picked up this book. When one person changes, the entire relationship changes.

One

TAKE A DEEP LOOK WITHIN

One of my (Katie's) first memories of learning to shift blame took place in Mrs. Guiton's second-grade class at Clover Elementary. I can remember sitting halfway back, right side of the classroom, when the teacher announced we had to immediately turn in our homework from the night before, placing our papers in a small plastic tub she would be passing around.

For the prior few weeks, she had been asking us to simply check off *yes* or *no* on a sheet of paper each day to say whether we had completed our homework. I had begun lying about it and was baffled that some students would check the no box. Why would they choose honesty in a moment that was so easy to skirt past? This daily silent act showed what little integrity and maturity I had, but it wasn't hurting anyone. And I had so much free time each night as I did less and less homework. I felt okay about this until that moment when my teacher passed around that plastic tub.

I decided to put my name and the date on an assignment I had completed the week prior, and I confidently submitted it. As an eight-year-old, I somehow realized I could go home and complete the homework that night, and when my teacher informed me I put the wrong paper in, I could easily claim, "Oh man, how did that get in there? I meant to give you this one." Sadly, the plan worked, and it sealed my path. I learned to own up to as little as possible to save face and not have to disappoint others with my wrongs. I continued this pattern well into high school, when I could have medaled in blame shifting and avoiding responsibility for my bad choices. This was difficult because my mother caught me red-handed many times, but it did not keep me from attempting it. I remember spending so much emotional energy trying to rebel and do what I wanted while trying to save face and seem like a "good girl."

In college, once I became a Christian, I was transformed from the inside out in a lot of ways. Many of my poor character traits were replaced by new qualities such as servanthood, joy, peace, and generosity. God definitely did a work in me and turned my life around. So you may be wondering how someone who loved God and sought after Him could also do something so sinful and selfish as have an affair. But like most people's faith stories, not everything changes overnight, and I was tempted by some tendencies that led me to behaviors of betrayal and shifting blame or responsibility to someone else.

When Josh and I first got married, any season of discontentment I was struggling with became Josh's fault. We chose to have a large family, and early on that came with the sacrifice of spending my younger years raising children while also working to grow my career as a school counselor. There was not a lot of margin in my life, and even though we chose this together, I resented having to work full-time and still carry the load of homemaker. In some seasons Josh got to go work while I had to stay home; he was able to travel while I was at home taking care of kids. Because I sacrificed what I wanted to do, selflessly serving our family, I blamed Josh for all my discontentment, rage, jealousy, frustration—you name it. At the end of the day, my ability to shift blame wreaked havoc on our marriage. As a master of deflecting responsibility, I admitted little to no sins, nor did I own any part of our life that wasn't working.

PERSONAL CHANGE CLEARS THE PATH FORWARD

Have you ever found yourself in cycles of blame? It's hard to get at the root issues and find solutions as a couple when your eyes are narrowly focused on your spouse and all the problems he or she is bringing to the table. Letting my mind go to places of discontent with my life or jealousy of another couple led me to worse places.

When I first recognized I was having an emotional affair, I developed ways to justify thinking of a future with another man. Disregarding all the warnings the Holy Spirit was giving me, I continued to argue in my mind a case against Josh to create more distance from him in my heart. Every time I felt sin and shame, I shifted the blame toward him, sometimes inwardly but often outwardly. Looking back, I can't believe all the ways I found fault in him, often thinking, *Josh works too hard and never makes time for me* or, *He doesn't value me or the kids*. I even went so far as letting him know I was convinced he had feelings for other women.

My story may sound ludicrous considering the very real sin in my heart, but Josh and I have discovered this scenario to be true for many couples we have walked with through their marriage crises. Shifting the focus to your partner is a habit that is formed quickly and sometimes even subconsciously when unhealthy patterns begin. When our friend left our house that night in tears, it was the first time I came face-to-face with the reality of what *my* sin and selfishness were causing not only for me and Josh but for another couple as well. When I confessed to Josh that night, even though only partially at the time, it was enough to know that I had betrayed his trust and our vows and was heading down the path of wanting out of our marriage completely.

I thought this alarming night for Josh and me would remain between the two of us, but it quickly became very public. As I look back on that time now, fifteen years later, I can see what a gift the public aspect of our story was to me, who had over the years achieved the heights of masterful manipulation, deception, and blame shifting. It's hard to maintain that posture when your crisis is out in the open.

Most people understand that while there may be problems in a marriage, real growth opportunities can never justify betrayal or giving your heart and love to someone besides your spouse. Whether you are currently in the middle of a mess or you're seeing potential problems, the most important first step in the process of growth and change is to start with yourself—a simple statement that is so much easier said than done.

Starting with yourself in the work of marriage can sometimes be the greatest mountain to climb before you'll ever see real changes. It requires a great deal of trust that correcting some of your patterns, behaviors, and unhealthy tendencies will lead to changing your marriage. Most people today do not believe that when they change themselves, they change their relationships. We have been conditioned to believe that it's others who control our feelings, emotions, paths, and outcomes. In a culture focused on happiness, people have unknowingly crafted marriages built on happy or pleasant emotions, and we learn early on to rely on—actually, *expect*—our spouse to satisfy, complete, or fulfill us.

When I was forced to start with me—to look inward, to

see my sin in our situation and acknowledge both publicly and privately the part I played in a marriage on the verge of breakdown—it didn't look textbook at first, but these things rarely do. I began by confessing to Josh that I had been thinking about another couple's life and love story for a while and how much better it seemed than the one we were living.

Often over time, seeds of doubt and discontentment with what God is doing in our lives can grow to all-out sin. We begin questioning whether our spouse or even God knows what's best for us. When it came to my happiness, I was pretty sure this was something I needed to author myself if Josh wasn't going to provide it. Well, in part I was right, and yet I still continued to place too much responsibility on Josh for my happiness. The truth is, for any of us to see real changes in our contentment, joy, or even happiness, it starts with our own soul and figuring out which of our needs we are wrongfully expecting others to fulfill.

I'll never forget what Josh told me when I confessed that I didn't know whether I loved him anymore and that I wanted something more: "Katie, I am asking you to go to a new place of love with me." Initially, I couldn't comprehend this concept, but I knew he believed in it, and that was just enough to help me understand I needed to be honest about where I was. I started to consider the destination of the path I was on—the pain of divorce, the pain for my children, and the end story with a new man. I realized that at the end of this story would be me, and if I was discontent with a man who loved me, what would prevent this from happening again?

"WHAT IF IT'S ME?"

The night that I wondered aloud to Josh, "What if it's me?" I asked myself the same question. When I forced myself to answer, I was choosing to address something much deeper: What if the only person I can change in this marriage is me? What if that would be enough? Starting with me, I began to acknowledge that I might be believing some really big lies about love, lust, and obsession rather than trusting what Scripture points to as love and God's intention for marriage. I was filled with shame for these emotions—not only in this season but for years to come—but God started to break those chains of sin, especially by showing me how this pattern of believing lies, shifting blame, and hiding from the real issues started with creation's first couple.

If anyone had a chance to get marriage right, it should have been Adam and Eve, who walked with God and enjoyed communion with Him. No distraction from others, no culture creating a different narrative on love. There was no sexual sin, addiction, or family drama. No *Bachelor* series! There was just them, yet they still found themselves in a marriage breakdown.

In Genesis 3, right at the start of creation, we find our sweet Eve getting the first doubts about the goodness of God. Satan presented her with the idea of disobedience, making sure the fruit on that tree looked especially enticing that day.

Now the serpent was more crafty than any other beast of the field that the LORD God had made. He said to the

9

woman, "Did God actually say, 'You shall not eat of any tree in the garden'?" And the woman said to the serpent, "We may eat of the fruit of the trees in the garden, but God said, 'You shall not eat of the fruit of the tree that is in the midst of the garden, neither shall you touch it, lest you die.'" But the serpent said to the woman, "You will not surely die. For God knows that when you eat of it your eyes will be opened, and you will be like God, knowing good and evil." So when the woman saw that the tree was good for food, and that it was a delight to the eyes, and that the tree was to be desired to make one wise, she took of its fruit and ate, and she also gave some to her husband who was with her, and he ate. Then the eyes of both were opened, and they knew that they were naked. And they sewed fig leaves together and made themselves loincloths. (vv. 1–7 ESV)

Did God really say?
Surely you won't die from doing your own thing.
The fruit looks so good and delightful and will make me wise.

Have you ever been there? You start to disbelieve ever so slightly what God has said, what He has called you to, and what He could do through your obedience. The fruit of doing your own thing can be more enticing than any of us realize until we are in a crisis-mode situation that prompts us to ask questions. Maybe you would ask the same questions I did all those years ago: *Will I lose my salvation if I leave my marriage?* The answer is no. *Will I really die if I chase happiness?* The answer may have been no, at least not immediately, but who knew long term, considering my road seemed like an endless, unsatisfying path toward destruction.

The labor of starting with yourself—that is, being exposed, putting in the emotional work, and cultivating your own garden—may seem too intensive and without a lot of payoff. Besides, the fruit of a new path seems so enticing and pleasurable, and maybe even wise from the world's point of view. Just do what you want, follow your own path, be fully known and loved, and enjoy the way God has made you to love multiple times and feel what you feel. Worldly wisdom, even if it's just slightly twisted from the truth of God's Word, is enough to lead us straight to places of death and destruction.

IF I TRUST HIM, IS HE GOOD?

I wish I could say this crisis in our marriage was the only time I have walked down this path of doubting God, doubting the goodness of the husband He gave me and the promise of what God could do with our right action and obedience. But there are so many small ways I can get back into this pattern of doubt and discontentment and be tempted to shift the focus of my blame to Josh. Thankfully I have learned that the more fruitful path out of a funk—which may last only hours but could last weeks—is to start with me. For me this looks like waking up and giving time and attention to talking to God about where I am and where I want to go. I open up to Him about all my dirty junk, then open His Word, expecting to hear from Him.

God is not silent, and He will speak to you if you will incline your ear to Him. When you pray, be honest about the real state of what you're feeling—disappointment, jealousy, frustration, discontentment, whatever. Nothing you tell Him will be a shock, since He already knows your every concern, but He wants to walk with you through these difficult times. Then step back and look more closely at the external things that you know are keeping you from communion with God. Maybe you are not spending time with Him, not getting enough sleep, not exercising enough, or are so busy that you have no time to breathe.

For me, allowing margin so I'm not full of stress is important. So is putting on my calendar things that I can look forward to or goals I'm working toward. There have been some seasons when I felt as if I could not break free from the blame cycle, when God clearly conveyed to me, *Let Josh off the hook.* This would prompt me to try an experiment: I would set a specific time frame, and during this period I would not blame Josh for anything. I would feel what I felt and get through it without making it about him or his issues. These seasons have shocked me each time as I realized three or four days later that I was seeing things differently and was able to see how starting with me gave me a healthy state of mind.

I want you to discover yourself and know what helps you feel peace, experience joy, and walk with more freedom and pep in your step. Admitting that this is not your spouse's job is a huge part of starting with you. Just know that seasons change, and what you need to feel satisfied can change too, so commit to studying yourself and the habits that tend to make you feel full and whole. Usually, if I will commit time to working on my own emotions and funk, I will hear from God about any lie I am believing or sin that I need to confess or repent of. And then I experience what Scripture promises: "Repent, then, and turn to God, so that your sins may be wiped out, that times of refreshing may come from the Lord" (Acts 3:19).

When starting with me, one of the more surprising things that came from our story happened one morning when I got up early to have time with God. While on the outside I was trying to do the right things—stay in the marriage and work to be accountable and earn Josh's trust back—internally I was still a mess. I told God I was "dying on the vine." I remember confessing to God, "I still just don't see all the great qualities in Josh." I knew they were there, but his personality still seemed so contrary to what I desired. I had seen other "fruit" and was considering how that personality seemed to fit so much better with mine. It's crazy to think how blinded I was to these lies, but in the moment it was hard to tell up from down. I needed the voice of God to sort out the lies and start seeing the truth.

One morning in particular I felt that God told me to open my eyes to Josh and study him again, to take a second look. I was unsure of how to do this, but that afternoon I went to the library and a book caught my eye. It was an older book by Tim LaHaye called *Spirit-Controlled Temperament*. God used that book to start a breakthrough as I began to study what type of temperament Josh had and what made him tick. I learned more about myself and my own weaknesses and the things that were growth opportunities in me. Sure enough, as God would have it, a lot of my weak spots were strengths in Josh. I began to see that when I focused first on my own weaknesses and used Josh's strengths to sharpen those, I felt differently about his habits and tendencies that had once seemed insurmountable to me.

All of this was in a time when I was tempted to throw in the towel because there were so many mountains standing before me, and looking inward was the last thing I wanted to do. But when I spent time with God, He helped me to pause and look inside. I started believing that through repentance I could get up, keep climbing those mountains, and not feel overcome by shame.

We have an enemy who is at war with our souls, and I believe he uses multiple tactics to make us feel discouraged, defeated, and full of shame so we feel stuck and unable to change. If I could encourage you with anything, it would be not to let him win between your ears. Seeking to hear God's voice and to see with His vision will help you to start with you and begin doing the work that brings about major changes in your life and marriage.

As much as I wish I could take credit for starting with me and initiating the restoration and growth of our marriage, God was moving through Josh as well. It's still a miracle to me that Josh also intuitively decided to start with himself, to do his own work in this process.

THE PATH TO AN ABUNDANT LIFE

I'm sure Mrs. Guiton never gave another thought about that day when I lied and turned in a previously finished assignment. But for more than thirty years it has never left my mind. We take us with us. The choices, sin, struggles, failures, and victories. Even in marriage, you are bringing together two people who are very much individuals with unique stories and journeys. If we don't start with us and learn how to do the work of introspection and self-reflection, we can't grow into our full potential and experience a life of abundance. God has uniquely wired us, made us in His image as the only one of us on this planet. You are an individual who is on a journey with Christ, and He wants to lead you on the path to an abundant life.

In order for your marriage to weather the hard days, thrive on ordinary days, and experience moments of exuberant joy, you must start with you. What does that work look like in the journey you are on? Have you looked at your marriage or circumstance from the perspective of what needs to change or grow in you instead of what should change in your spouse? What things could you do behaviorally, emotionally, or spiritually that would bring about a change in the entire relationship?

If the best way for God to do the miraculous in your marriage starts with you, ask Him what that would look like. There is too much at risk not to put all your trust in Him. Josh and I believe in you both and are confident that by starting with you and committing to the journey, you will see God do a miracle only He can take credit for!

As we get started on this journey to help you S.T.A.Y. in your marriage, it's going to take God's strength as we humble ourselves and desire to look more like a reflection of His love. Will you take this moment to pray with me for Him to do a new work in you individually?

Lord, I commit to starting with me. You say You oppose the proud and give grace to the humble, and that's my ask—would You humble me and allow me to see things I may have missed? Open my eyes to the changes I can make that will bring about more life and abundance in my marriage. Give me the strength to obey the things You are calling me to. I am putting all my trust in You. I surrender and commit to doing my own work as I stay.

Two

"FATHER, FORGIVE THEM"

D o you remember your wedding vows? Real talk: I just asked Katie if she remembered ours—because I don't. In fact, when I think back on our wedding day, the majority of it is a blur. We had dated for two years, were engaged for fourteen months, and had gone through premarital counseling. So much of the ceremony felt like a formality. It felt like a finish line we'd crossed, fulfilling a long season of waiting and dreaming. At the same time, it was a starting point, where dreams would become reality. I remember the date, the location, the decorations, and many of the friends and family who chose to make the drive and show up a couple of days before Christmas. All of which are special and important. But I don't recall our vows. Do you remember yours?

It seems kind of crazy, right? When you buy a home, you know the terms: the interest rate, the number of years it will be financed, and what the monthly payment will be. Your commitment is to make regular payments for a defined period of time. But when entering into the covenant of marriage, the terms are not determined by the market, the lender, or your credit. The terms are established by God, and the expectations and agreement are the same for every couple.

Since reciting our vows, I've officiated more than one hundred weddings over the past twenty years. Though some couples write and recite their own vows, most couples choose traditional vows similar to the ones below. This is one of the examples I recommend to couples:

I, [name], take you, [name], to be my wedded [husband/wife], to have and to hold from this day forward, for better, for worse, for richer or for poorer, in sickness and in health, to love and to cherish, 'til death do us part, according to God's ordinance; and thereto I pledge thee my troth.

"Worse" hit me like a truck in the night. I was not only betrayed but blindsided. It's one thing when you have suspicions—when things don't feel right, don't seem to be lining up, and you find yourself questioning your spouse's whereabouts, not trusting their responses—but I experienced none of that. Things had been hard, but that was largely our own fault. We were starting a family, getting our master's degrees, renovating homes, acquiring rental property, and working full-time jobs. The struggle was real, but we were getting through it. I classified the tension, frustration, and arguments as normal. We were a young couple trying to figure out how to carry it all. That's part of what made the reality of an affair so painful. I realized that not only could I not trust Katie and not trust my friend, but I couldn't even trust myself. I thought I knew where we were and how we were doing, but this season taught me why "How are we doing as a couple?" is always a question that should lead to a conversation and never a foregone conclusion—because you may very well be wrong.

We could have made new friends, left that neighborhood, found new jobs, or moved to a new city. We could have changed everything about our lives on the outside. But the greatest challenge of all wasn't on the outside. It was inside us.

In that season, "worse" wasn't financial, professional, or medical. It was emotional. What could I do with my anger, bitterness, pain, and sadness? I could trust God with the relationship. I had seen Him heal and restore. I had faith that He could heal and fix all the stuff people can see. But could He bring about real-time change in me? It seemed impossible as I experienced sporadic crying fits and an uncontrollable thought life that seemed more like a movie reel. I constantly envisioned the things Katie had confessed, and my thoughts and feelings were running wild. In trying to manage it all, I couldn't stuff it, medicate it, run from it, or avoid it. It was a ton of bricks that sat on my chest. The pain of betrayal dominated my emotions, consumed my thoughts, and shaped my actions. I wasn't leaving, but I also wasn't living. I was stuck.

THE HARD TRUTH ABOUT FORGIVENESS

DJ Khaled has always been one of my favorite artists. He's a funny guy. He has lots of personality, dances kind of goofy, is crazy confident, and is wildly successful. I follow him on Instagram, listen to all his music, and regularly watch videos that he releases online. As a DJ, the majority of his success comes through partnerships with some of the best artists in the industry: Jay-Z, Beyoncé, Drake, Bieber, and the list goes on and on. When talking about his success, he'll often say, "Major key alert . . . major key alert," upon which he'll drop some knowledge that was "a key to his success."[1] I hear his voice in my head when I hear something helpful or pick up a leadership lesson I need to hold on to. That said (major key alert!), a lesson on forgiveness is how God silenced the crazy in me and ushered Katie and me into a new season.

I realize how that may land on you: hard. Especially if you've been hurt. I don't pretend to understand your circumstances, and I'm not minimizing your pain. Forgiveness may feel like the furthest thing from your reach right now. I get it. I felt the same way. But be encouraged: this is a work that God can do in you, not something you have to manufacture on your own. There is no forgiveness switch you can flip in your heart or mind. But God can bring about the new feelings, thoughts, and reality to unlock the places you feel stuck.

After all, your feelings often follow your feet. You may need to start walking a road that leads to trusting God to bring about feelings you can't muster up yet. I am not saying feelings are the end game or that you should "fake it till you feel it." I hate the sound of that, and chances are your spouse does too. What I mean is, predecide how you are going to treat your spouse in the face of betrayal. Or just in the face of him or her doing something that bothers you. This is something you do when reciting your vows—"for better or for worse"—but it's also something you have to remind yourself of when confronted with worse.

Jesus modeled this while sharing the Last Supper with the disciples, reclining at the table with the Twelve. "And while they were eating, he said, 'Truly I tell you, one of you will betray me'" (Matt. 26:21). Just a few verses later, we read that Jesus knew it was going to be Judas (v. 25). Yet in that moment, instead of confronting, challenging, or outing him to the other disciples—He served him Communion. Jesus made the decision to love and serve Judas with full knowledge of his future betrayal. To present him with the bread and the cup, symbolic of His body that would be given and His blood that would be shed.

You may not be a sellout or a liar, but you are a sinner.

One of the primary motivators to help you forgive is remembering that Jesus' posture toward Judas is the same one He's taken toward you. Starting here, in your moments of greatest pain, allows the knowledge of your need for forgiveness to become something you can experience emotionally. Feeling the weight of betrayal, the heartbreaking, soul-crushing emptiness, gives us a glimpse into what Jesus took on Himself. He paid the price for my sin, He chose to love and forgive me, and because of that, we can forgive others.

So how do we do that? Jesus gives us a pretty clear picture in Luke 23. This is the passage God used to help me walk out forgiveness and take me to a new place emotionally while I waited on Him to restore our marriage. This verse captures Jesus' final prayer before His death. He prayed, "Father, forgive them, for they do not know what they are doing." The rest of that verse reads, "And they divided up his clothes by casting lots" (v. 34). It goes on in verse 35 to say, "The people stood watching, and the rulers even sneered at him. They said, 'He saved others; let him save himself if he is God's Messiah, the Chosen One.'" It sounds like they knew exactly what they were doing. They had stripped, beaten, and crucified the man who came to save them. Yet in the moment of His greatest pain, His prayer was that we might experience the forgiveness of God.

God used this prayer to bring about change in my life, and I'm praying that He uses it and the revelation He gave me to do the same in you. Here are three thoughts that may help you.

1. Stay Focused

In seasons of pain, the "me" filter is strong. When I am hurting, when my future is uncertain, when my relationship is broken, when my world is shattered, or when I'm out of time, the focus is always on me. Maybe your health, employment, finances, or children's education are in question, and you are asking, "What am I going to do?" or "How do I handle this?" When our thoughts, questions, and focus turn inward, our world gets very small. Given Jesus' circumstances, you'd think He would have prayed, "Comfort Me, Father. Give Me strength. Give Me courage. Heal My body." I can think of a thousand things I would have prayed, most of which would have been for me.

But not Jesus; He was on a mission. His name is Jesus Christ, and it's important to note that *Christ* was not His last name. In fact, it's not a name at all but a title. It is the Greek word *Christos*, which translates to the Hebrew word *Mashiach*, or Messiah, meaning "the Anointed One."[2] Jesus is the Anointed One, our Messiah, our Savior. Luke 19:10 tells us that Jesus came on the greatest rescue mission of all time, "to seek and to save the lost." Up until His last breath, Jesus was focused on the mission. He did not allow His momentary pain to overshadow His eternal purpose.

In the midst of our pain, this is what we often do. It can feel impossible to think about the rest of our lives when we're having a hard time getting through the rest of the day. Things like eternity, the mission, our dreams, or the generational impact of our decisions can get sacrificed in light of today's pain. In the midst of heartbreak, we have to remember that we do have an enemy, but it is not our spouse. When you find yourself experiencing the worst days in your marriage, stay focused. Don't let your worst days be your last.

2. Pray for God's Best, Even When You See Their Worst

After Katie confessed her affair, it took her some time to fully sever the relationship she was having. It was almost like a drug. Because she had been sneaking around, the relationship brought about some degree of anticipation, mystery, and excitement. She was having real feelings, endorphins were being released, stuff was happening inside her—it just wasn't God-honoring. I believed she wanted to stay. I sincerely thought she wanted to choose me and our family. Yet she struggled to be honest with me or to tell me the whole truth. In that season, it felt as if the Lord was fighting for me. He'd tell me to go to her office, sit in her car, check her phone, or take some other action. Part of me felt crazy. Always questioning things while trying to establish trust was exhausting. Nonetheless, God would position me to intercept a note, see a text, stop her from meeting him somewhere, or do something else.

One day, we were at her mom's house, hanging out at the neighborhood pool. I'd walked back to the car to get my sunglasses. As I sat in the driver's seat, her phone pinged. A text had come through from a random number. I realized they were still communicating. I stepped out of the car and shouted her name. She got in the car, and we drove to the other side of the parking lot. I remember screaming, "Do you not fear God?" There seemed to be no driving conviction in her to stop the destructive behavior. I could make no sense of it. We'd made some significant strides; I thought we were in a better place. I was wrong, and it was crushing. I knew it could get worse: she could leave. But since she was with me still(-ish), it was hard to imagine things getting worse.

In that season, God started speaking to me in prayer. Not about me, my pain, anxiety, or discouragement, but about who He created Katie to be. Katie's full name is Katherine Elizabeth. Katherine means "pure" in Greek, and Elizabeth is a Hebrew name meaning "God is my oath." God gave me a glimpse of her from His eyes, which changed my feelings. He had created her with a pure heart. In this season, my battle was not about her faithfulness to me but about her faithfulness to Him. It was about her seeing herself for who He created her to be and stepping into the life He had called her to. Somehow, those words in prayer took away the sting from the offenses. That season in prayer lowered the walls of the "me" filter and allowed my prayers to be about God's plans for her. Her future, her health, His dreams for her, His will to be done.

In the face of betrayal, while being mocked by those He came to seek and save, Jesus prayed for God's best: "Father, forgive them." What is interesting about the forgiveness of God is that, unlike earthly fathers, it is not an expression of His character but an expense of the cross. In order to forgive our sin as a holy God, a price had to be paid. It was from the cross, the place of His greatest pain, where this transaction would be paid in full. He took my sin on Himself, making it possible for me to have a relationship with God. When we experience His love, when we receive His forgiveness, it puts our pain in perspective and gives us access to the power of prayer.

3. Remember That What They Do Is Not Who They Are

We live in a world that says, "If it walks like a duck and quacks like a duck . . . it's a duck." People are the summation of their actions. Regardless of your intentions, culturally you will be judged by what you do. So here's a question for you: Are you a sinner or a saint?

If you are anything like me, you struggle daily with sin. Some of which is in my heart and mind, some of which is manifested in the way I treat my kids, talk to my wife, or respond to people who drive me crazy. You could look at me and say, "Josh is a sinner." Which is true—but that is not who I really am. I am a new creation; the old has gone, and the new has come (2 Cor. 5:17). I am not my own; I was bought at a price. I am a child of God.

All throughout Paul's letters, he addressed people as God saw them, not as their actions reflected. In his letter to the Ephesians, he wrote that the people there were struggling with immorality and impurity, yet he addressed them as "the saints who are in Ephesus" (1:1 NKJV). In the book of

Romans, Paul spoke directly about the daily struggle with sin to a people who were feeling social pressures, tension, and frustration among believers, yet he addressed the letter "to all who are beloved of God in Rome, called as saints" (1:7 NASB). Your story—and my story—is no different. You may have lied, you may have cheated, or those things may have happened to you. Whatever the case, in order to forgive yourself or your spouse, remember that who they are is not what they do. Those labels sneak into our hearts and minds in time of idle thought. They come out in our words in the midst of arguments. We have to check our thoughts and watch our words to ensure we are thinking, praying, and speaking to who they are in Christ, not to who we define them as based on their actions.

Have you ever stubbed your toe in the dark? Imagine standing there, holding your foot in pain, while someone yelled at you because of the stupidity of your actions. That would make no sense. When we deviate from the will and way of God in our lives, we're no better off than someone walking around with the lights off, only bringing about pain to ourselves and others. Regardless of your personality, skill set, success, confidence, or competence, you can't manage the outcomes of deeds done in the dark. It's a slippery slope that leads to death.

Jesus prayed that God would forgive those who were crucifying Him, knowing that their behavior and actions were those of a people walking around in the dark. Even godly people can find themselves in dark places. Your spouse may have hurt you in ways that you'd never imagined. But remember, no one can make reasonable decisions in the dark. Who they are is not what they do.

⁓

At some point in marriage, you'll experience the anger, brokenness, and pain of "worse." You'll finally understand what those vows mean. But don't let that scare you. Just by having picked up this book, there's a good chance you've already tasted moments of it. Your story may be similar to ours. You may have experienced a prolonged season of rebuilding and establishing trust. Or you may have experienced some drift, things aren't feeling better, and you're concerned about where you're headed. Whatever the case, you're not alone. And this is a critical moment.

The couples that persevere through the worst of marriage to get to the best of marriage have one other thing in common. It's not just that they've experienced the worst; every couple gets there. It's that they've chosen to forgive. Remind yourself of the vows you exchanged, even if you can't recite them. Feel the weight of those words and allow God to do the needed work in you to help you walk them out.

Three

WORSHIP IS
WARFARE

hat's my jam!

You may have never used those words, but we've all shared the feeling of excitement when "my song" came on. Maybe you were driving up the road and found yourself singing it out loud, or you were casually talking at a wedding reception when the DJ turned it on and you *had* to hit the dance floor, or you were about to go hard at the gym and pulled it up yourself to get you fired up. What is that song for you? For me (Josh), it's just about anything '90s hip-hop. Some of you can relate.

My life looks nothing like Snoop Dogg's these days, but throw on anything he, Dr. Dre, or Tupac released in the '90s, and I can recite the words as if I'd learned them yesterday. Isn't it interesting how that works? Certain song lyrics find their way into our long-term memory, primarily because of the impact they've had on us. The music may have been associated with a milestone moment or played frequently throughout a season of your life. Often, the lyrics communicate thoughts or feelings we'd like to express that we may not have had the words for. These songs have a way of narrowing our focus; it's hard to sing and dance to one of your favorites while at the same time feeling the stresses of the day.

I remember the day *Totally Krossed Out* was released by Kris Kross in 1992. I may or may not have pretended to be sick the day after I picked it up. The lyrics of each song were printed on the cover sleeve of the CD. I remember reading them and singing along to my favorites on repeat until I had memorized the words. The same could be said for many of the songs on Michael Jackson's *Dangerous* album in 1991 or Craig Mack's *Project: Funk da World* in 1994. What are those artists and albums and songs for you?

What's interesting about the songs I jammed to growing up, and secular music in general, is that their power is found in distracting us from whatever we may be walking through. When you throw on your jam, it will momentarily lift your spirits and allow you to sing and dance your way into or out of a mood, but it can never take you to a new place. Moments after the song ends, you are left to face your thoughts and emotions.

That's not the case with worship music. Where "my jam" is effective at distracting me, worship is effective at delivering me.

What does that mean? Physically, you may be in the same place; the problems are still present, the marriage is still difficult, the behaviors have yet to change, and the spouse has yet to return. Whatever the case, this season's circumstances may look the same. Worship, however, empowers us to wage war on the ways of this world, the attacks from our enemy, and our weak flesh in a way that can deliver us mentally, spiritually, and emotionally. I can't think things like, *It's over. I can't make her love me. Things are never going to change*, while I sing songs that profess to the Lord, "[You are my] way maker, miracle worker, promise keeper, light in the darkness. My God, that is who you are."[1] My thoughts and the lyrics to Sinach's "Way Maker" don't jibe. One is a feeling, and one is the truth. The former must submit to the latter. As real as our emotions seem, the reality of God's Word, His truth, takes precedence over the lies we may have convinced ourselves to believe. Worship has a way of grabbing us by the hand and helping us climb out of a dark place that makes us feel hopeless.

LIES OF THE ENEMY

When Jesus was led into the wilderness to be tempted by the devil, Scripture tells us that after fasting for forty days and forty nights, He was hungry. Let's first imagine for a moment how Jesus must have been feeling. The words that come to mind for me are *weak*, *lonely*, *tired*, and as the passage says, hungry. Do you remember the last time you simultaneously experienced some combination of those emotions? When you feel fatigued physically, mentally, emotionally, and spiritually because of the environment or season you are in, you have an increased likelihood of compromise—compromising your integrity, convictions, dreams, and desires for what will bring instant gratification. Jesus was in precisely this kind of vulnerable state when the Enemy came to tempt Him:

> After fasting forty days and forty nights, he was hungry. The tempter came to him and said, "If you are the Son of God, tell these stones to become bread." Jesus answered, "It is written: 'Man shall not live on bread alone, but on every word that comes from the mouth of God.'" Then the devil took him to the holy city and had him stand on the highest point of the temple. "If you are the Son of God," he said, "throw yourself down. For it is written: 'He will command his angels concerning you, and they will lift you up in their hands, so that you will not strike your foot against a stone.'" Jesus answered him, "It is also written: 'Do not put the Lord your God to the test.'" Again, the devil took him to a very high mountain and showed him all the kingdoms of the world and their splendor. "All this I will give you," he said, "if you will bow down and worship me." Jesus said to him, "Away from me, Satan! For it is written: 'Worship the Lord your God, and serve him only.'" Then the devil left him, and angels came and attended him. (Matt. 4:2–11)

Just as it was true for Jesus, it is in these moments when our willingness to worship reveals what we believe to be true and helps us wage war against the Enemy. He'd love to convince you that your marriage is over, your spouse won't change, and that the two of you will never get to a new place. He'd love for you to believe the lies he's whispering are your reality, that the problems are in some way more significant than the object of our praise. But when we are squeezed, when the pressure is on, our worship has a way of positioning God above our problems. Worship gives us a new narrative; it helps us declare the truth, giving us both a language and a melody to fight with when we feel hopeless and defeated.

IDLE MOMENTS

Idle moments were the most difficult. I'd be driving up the road, lying in bed moments before falling asleep, or having a thirty-minute window at work between meetings when there was no specific task to complete. It's almost as if I would subconsciously ponder my pain and watch our story unfold on a movie screen in my mind. Katie had confessed so much, from minor details to deep betrayal and the reality of her thoughts and feelings. All these were foundational in building trust; I went from being in the dark to being in the know. However, her confession fueled my imagination with questions. *Is that all she did? What did that look like? When? Where?* Upon which my mind would get to work putting the movie together.

Character development, the scene, the script—before I knew it, I was driving up the road, white-knuckling the steering wheel, enraged. I remember countless times being minutes into a scene, having worked up feelings that were as fresh as if the betrayal had just happened, only to have a moment of clarity where I'd realize my thoughts were out of control and catalyzing pain. I'd shake my head and say aloud, "What are you doing?" confronting the fact that my thoughts were hurting me, not helping me.

Have you ever been there?

Often, the spaces in between have few distractions—the drive between work and home for example. Have you ever found yourself sitting in traffic, thinking about the day? It's natural to find yourself replaying conversations, trying to interpret the look on someone's face, what they meant by what they said, what you wish you had said, or the way an email read. The spaces in between allow your thoughts to run rampant, processing places of uncertainty and working to reconcile places of pain. Medical research suggests that our brains respond to emotional and physical pain in almost the same way.[2] If you cut yourself while doing the dishes, you wouldn't question whether a response was appropriate. You'd likely scream, grab your hand, maybe shed some tears. The pain would elicit a response involuntarily. Emotional wounds, however, are invisible. We have a way of hiding, managing, and distracting ourselves from dealing with them, but when we are presented with idle moments, our minds work involuntarily to make sense of and resolve our emotional wounds.

It would be nice if, when presented with a painful thought or experiencing a negative emotion, all we had to do is push a button that changes the channel. Channel up, channel down, track down, power off, whatever the case . . . I want to see, think, and feel something different. Unfortunately, that's often not the case. Distracting ourselves from painful emotions only delays dealing with them; the feelings are sure to return. It takes both time and intentionality to redirect your thoughts, but the good news is that we aren't powerless in the process.

In 2 Corinthians 10:3–5, the apostle Paul said this: "For though we live in the world, we do not wage war as the world does. The weapons we fight with are not the weapons of the world. On the contrary, they have the divine power to demolish strongholds. We demolish arguments and every pretension that sets itself up against the knowledge of God, and we take captive every thought to make it obedient to Christ."

Our "weapons" have "divine power to demolish strongholds." In the New Testament, that phrase was originally written in Greek as *kathairesin ochyromaton* and implies the ability to overcome resistance and break through barriers. The root word of that phrase is *ochuromu*, which references arguments used during a debate.[3] In other words, Paul was saying that we have access to spiritual weapons that empower us to overcome the physical and intellectual attacks of the Enemy. Not to merely defend ourselves against them but to demolish them! The question then is, What are these weapons and how do I fight back?

ARMED FOR BATTLE
WITH AIRPODS

In my darkest season, worship was my preferred weapon of warfare. There were countless nights where we'd get in bed, Katie would quickly fall asleep with her back turned toward me, and I would lie there in the dark with my questions and fears. *Will she ever love me again? Will this ever get better? Is she still communicating with him? Is there anything I don't know? What will our future hold?* Often, late at night, the primary emotion I'd experience was profound sadness. I'd lie there crying, broken over the fact that her heart felt so far from me, though she was physically close. The pain of betrayal, the lack of intimacy, the loneliness, and the uncertainty about our future hurt so bad. But in those moments when my thoughts and feelings felt out of control, I could put in my AirPods, turn on some worship music, and allow it to wash over me until the power of the lyrics brought peace to my pain.

In the darkness of night, I didn't need my Bible, journal, a pen, or a light to go after God. It didn't require any effort on my part other than turning the music on. Upon which the Spirit of God would show up to comfort and encourage me until I'd fall asleep. I woke up so many mornings with terrible earaches, having rolled over in the night and slept with my AirPods in.

There are other weapons we need to engage in warfare. For example, Hebrews 4:12 says, "For the word of God is alive and active. Sharper than any double-edged sword, it penetrates even to dividing soul and spirit, joints and marrow; it judges the thoughts and attitudes of the heart." Spending time in God's Word can help you discern the truth from the lies. It presents a positive and life-giving narrative to the monologue you may be reciting internally that is loaded with lies and leads to places of death.

Philippians 4:6–7 says, "Do not be anxious about anything, but in every situation, by prayer and petition, with thanksgiving, present your requests to God. And the peace of God, which transcends all understanding, will guard your hearts and minds in Christ Jesus." Amid my worry, anxiety, and fear about the future of our marriage, I came to Him over and over. I do not doubt that God was actively at work pursuing Katie and restoring us even when I didn't see it or feel it, because of the power of prayer.

I spent countless hours reading God's Word and crying out to Him in prayer. But listening to worship music was the weapon that I found to be most effective in helping me "take captive every thought to make it obedient to Christ." Paul's language in this passage is militant. He was waging war, attacking his thoughts and forcing them to submit to the truth, becoming obedient to Christ.

Imagine someone breaking into your house; they are free to steal things that belong to you, cause physical harm to you and those you love, or cause damage to your property. Until the trespasser is brought to submission by a greater power or authority, you are at risk of harm and subject to pain. The same is true with our thoughts. Until they have been taken captive and become obedient to Christ, we are at risk of harm and subject to pain. When your thoughts and emotions feel like an intruder who has come to bring harm, and you feel powerless in taking him captive, worship is the weapon that can help you.

Paul and Silas were severely flogged, thrown into prison, and put in the inner cell with their feet in the stocks. The text in Acts 16 doesn't indicate how they were doing emotionally or what kind of thoughts they were having. But imagine for a moment how you would feel. Physically, we know they were bruised and bloody. Flogging was a severe and systematic beating with whips, rods, and other items to inflict pain. If this were me, emotionally I'd feel powerless, fearful of my future, and angry because of how I'd been treated. Paul and Silas were people just like you and me; indeed, they experienced the gamut of emotions. But then we see their preferred weapon of warfare:

About midnight Paul and Silas were praying and singing hymns to God, and the other prisoners were listening to them. Suddenly there was such a violent earthquake that the foundations of the prison were shaken. At once all the prison doors flew open, and everyone's chains came loose. The jailer woke up, and when he saw the prison doors open, he drew his sword and was about to kill himself because he thought the prisoners had escaped. But Paul shouted, "Don't harm yourself! We are all here!" (vv. 25–28)

It was the middle of the night; there was no electricity and likely no candle in their cell. They were tired, hurting, and bound in a dark place. In this moment every indicator would point to a physical battle: people, circumstances, guards, and shackles. But Paul knew the reality of Ephesians 6:12: "For our struggle is not against flesh and blood, but against the rulers, against the authorities, against the powers of this dark world and against the spiritual forces of evil in the heavenly realms."

Instead of focusing on the reality of their situation and giving way to their emotions, Paul and Silas turned to God, who is greater than them both. They were praying and singing hymns to God. Declaring His goodness, presence, and power and reminding themselves of God's incredible love for them and His faithfulness to them. In doing so, God didn't just change their attitudes or give them a fresh perspective. He shook the very foundations of the prison. Doors flew open and chains came loose, giving a physical expression of a spiritual reality.

When you are experiencing pain, feeling isolated, tired, and bound up, it's hard not to focus on yourself. But you are not a victim. You are not powerless. You may not be able to see a desired outcome or deliver yourself from your circumstances, but worship is the weapon to help you fight back and cry out to the God who can!

Four

CONFESSION
THERAPY

I (Katie) sat frozen in my chair when our friend walked out the door that night when my sin was exposed. I couldn't move. Time seemed to stop, and somehow, I knew that there were two choices before me. I only know now, looking back, that they were two paths—life or death. Honestly, what I felt at that moment was fear, guilt, sadness, and an overwhelmed feeling that I could not see the light or a way out of this nightmare I had created.

Even still, a frozen murmur is what happened next. Josh

got up to move and started to go back to whatever he was doing in the kitchen, probably thinking about what a terrible situation our friend and her husband were in. Instead, his ears caught those words that were barely audible from the other side of the room: "What if it's me?"

If you had told me that this tiny opening of my mouth, this slight murmur, was the crack in the cave, the little bit of light we needed to start to get out of the deep trap the Enemy was delighting himself in, I wouldn't have believed you.

That was the first and only thing I could get out at that moment. After six years of marriage, making love, having children, I had not yet crossed the line of what I now know is true intimacy. Until that night in the kitchen, I had never confessed anything of significance related to our marriage, at least not that I remember. Admitting to betrayal and an affair with our close friend was not the best ground on which to try out this new practice of confession. But it wasn't really me saying those four words—"What if it's me?"—it was the Holy Spirit in me, the heart of God somehow willing that thought out of my mouth.

From that moment on, I pretty much blanked out the rest of the night. I remember only Josh's eyes as he looked at me and began to understand the reality of what he might be facing. It was as if all his previous intuitions started playing back for him at that moment. He had been fighting against acknowledging how bad things had gotten between us, the depths of how much I could hurt and betray him. I know he wasn't allowing himself to believe it. But at that moment, I saw all of the truth and hurt coming to the surface in his eyes. When he asked, "What do you mean? Tell me more of what you mean," I couldn't. I wouldn't. I had not practiced for this sort of pain, humility, or nakedness. I wasn't ready to fully confess, and I think he knew that was all he was going to get from me, so out the door he went, running to our neighbors'.

He ran across the street to try to get more of the story. By the night's end, one thing was clear: there had been an inappropriate and devastating relationship, and things would never be the same in our marriages. We were shattered. The following day I began to tell Josh more about when the affair started and how it progressed. As he left to go to the church to meet with the lead pastor and his boss to bring this truth to light, I had been hopeful that what I shared with him would stay between us, but in God's grace, that is not how the story went. I say "by God's grace" because the path of great healing had to begin with the pastor in leadership asking Josh to step down and asking me never to walk back into that church.

REFINED BY FIRE

In chapter 3 of the book of Daniel, we read of three friends— Shadrach, Meshach, and Abednego—who refused to worship any gods but the one true God. When King Nebuchadnezzar threatened to throw them into a fire for this disobedience, they were not worried. They knew God was able to deliver them from any danger. But even more important, they told the king that should God decide not to deliver them from the fire, they would continue to worship Him.

The story goes on to tell about an angel joining them in the fire, and this image is meant to point to Jesus in our lives. Amid any trial you face, Jesus will either deliver you from it or join you in it. Often the delivery comes from the joining; the fire produces the freedom. This was the story for us and is often the truth of what occurs when the heat turns up in life because of confession. When we keep something hidden, any small or devastating thing, and there are no consequences, there is often no path to rebuild. The fire clears the way to bring new growth of trust and intimacy, but often in the moment, all you can see or feel is the burn or heat.

For our story, this was true during and after my confession, which became very public as pastors and leaders in the community shared with others an altered story that had many gaps. You know what happens when there are gaps in a story—people will seek to close them with their thoughts, opinions, or lies. In the school where I worked as a guidance counselor and which I loved so much, news spread like wildfire through parents and teachers. I will never forget catching people's glances and knowing immediately that they were processing my actions or, as many would do, judging me. Because I had so much shame personally, their judgmental thoughts and looks did not seem to bother me. It was almost as if they couldn't have come close to my thoughts of myself at this moment. Looking back, the interesting thing is that I know all this was for my good.

I remember vividly the night we drove to my in-laws' house for me to confess to them. I sat silently yet resolved that the only way forward was to bare the whole truth. When I looked into the eyes of Josh's father and mother and shared the story with them, the shock across their faces shook me to my core. I knew I had hurt them deeply in breaking their son. However, I will never forget that in the moments following my confession to Josh's parents and to my own parents, I felt closer to them than before. Somehow even in the pain of it, the confession brought intimacy with them. It was as if they knew me more profoundly than I knew myself and loved me unconditionally despite my behavior.

The same would hold true for Josh and me, although I didn't see it as quickly. Seeing the fuller picture now, I know that my confession was the first true act of intimacy we'd had in six to twelve months. So much hiding, pretending, and saving face wreaked havoc on our oneness. Confession was the foundation on which we'd build back that intimacy.

The truth about the fire of this moment for us was that the principles that Scripture paints using Daniel's story held true for us too. When the three friends were in the fire and the angel joined them, they came out unharmed. But something happened to them and changed them while they were there. When they went in, their arms and legs were bound with rope, but when they emerged from the fire, the rope was no longer attached.

The fire that confession brought in our darkest season of hopelessness changed both of us. We did not walk alone; there was a third. Not one day did we face the grief, shame, loneliness, anger, and pain alone. When the three of us walked out, some ropes that were binding us forever fell off. We learned in that season that honesty and bearing all before each other was our path to freedom. Saving face, the approval of others, behaving as though our marriage was perfect when it was not, would be burned from the confession of this trial.

> Therefore, confess your sins to one another and pray for one another, that you may be healed. The prayer of a righteous person has great power as it is working. (James 5:16 ESV)

When sin is confessed, healing can be ushered in. This promise of confession leading to healing has proved true for hundreds of couples we have met with. I understand only in part the spiritual, emotional, and physical truth of it, but I know that there are shame cycles within us—moving from sin to shame to guilt to sin again—that occur when we are hiding in sin. When confession happens, the second part of the cycle is broken. While you may feel shame before confession, once the shame is brought to the light and met by another person hearing and showing you love, the shame that seeks to isolate you is broken.

God does not want you to feel pain. Conviction or guilt that leads us to repentance is meant to bring us life. Shame is meant to bring us harm or death. Confession fights the battle against shame.

"I NEED TO TELL YOU SOMETHING HARD"

The truth is that all of us fall short. We all know this, but no one likes to admit it. In this season, Josh and I developed a habit of confession that was pivotal in leading us to increased trust and intimacy, not only in that season but in seasons to come, and still today.

As the months passed, I would start to remember another part of the sin or lies I had told Josh. Often it would be something that would seem insignificant, but I could feel myself thinking about it alone. That would trigger me to share it with Josh, even if it was something I'd already been forgiven of, because I knew the Enemy was bringing it up again to shame me. So I would say to Josh, "Hey, tonight, when the kids go down, I need to tell you something hard." This would prepare him for another confession. It became a habit that we called "confession therapy." It wasn't that there was no pain involved in hearing the truth, but it began to break the pattern of trying to save the relationship at the expense of honesty or the truth.

Speaking truth and being honest in love is the best we can hope for when it comes to intimacy. Speaking truth can be confessing a sin or talking about a fear you have, a feeling of hurt, or something you have been secretly worrying about. There are no rules on what is shared, just that if it's being tossed around in your mind, you are going to bring it to the light so it doesn't affect your oneness.

Being honest in love helps us be able to say something that is hard without it coming across as harsh. Something hard would be, "I have a fear about your physical health. Can we work on this together, or is there any way I can support you in meeting your goals?" This is a hard truth to speak out loud in a relationship, but if you love someone and want to grow old together, something must be said when the other spouse is not living healthily. Speaking the truth in love is not harshly saying, "Why can't you get it together regarding your health?" or any manner of other things that could hurt the person deeply.

The same is true for confession. One day I needed to tell Josh about a headband I had worn to impress the other man. "I wore this headband thinking he would like it. I want to get rid of it and this secret between us." That confession was challenging but not harsh. I had to tell Josh because I knew anything kept in the dark, any secret I withheld from him, would further divide us. We now practice confession therapy and tell each other anything we are struggling with in our minds, and it has changed our intimacy in more ways than I have space to write about.

THE HABIT AND THE REWARD

To create a habit in any area, we have found it helpful to have a language and a reward for the practice. So for confession—even now we use this same principle anytime we have to speak something hard to each other—we start with a language that says, "Can we have confession therapy tonight?" or "Hey, can I tell you something hard tonight?" Often before I start, I will also ask, "Can you handle me?" or "Can you handle my level 10?" This sets up the discussion with a commitment to the vows you have made to each other. I want to hear Josh say, in one way or another: "Of course I can handle you; this is marriage. It's not always easy, but it is supposed to be honest. This is what we signed up for, for better or worse, and we can tackle anything we know about together."

You cannot fight for something that is hidden. And anything hidden will fight against your marriage becoming stronger and healthier. Once you create the habit of telling each other the truth and are no longer willing to fight alone, then you need a reward. It's not going to be easy to hear or share with each other, but try to end the time with something like, "I am thankful you shared this with me." Even in your pain or possibly your lack of understanding a struggle your spouse has had, you must be able to say these words.

Then, I highly recommend you end your time praying together. Here is where the supernatural work comes in and when you realize you are not alone in the fight for your marriage.

FORGIVENESS IS A PRACTICE

Unity is God's idea, and when you invite Him into this process toward oneness, He will faithfully fulfill His promise in

James 5:16. Once you confess, you can believe your prayers will become more powerful, and healing will be yours. I think it's why the Enemy is so adamant about keeping your struggles, doubts, and sins in the dark—he knows Jesus' power is waiting on the other side of sharing the truth, and he wants to keep you in torment.

Confession doesn't come easy, and the process can be painful, but it gets easier as you faithfully address the damaged or neglected areas of your relationship and start rebuilding trust day by day, conversation by conversation. As you both move forward as flawed humans committed to disclosing the whole truth and making your marriage better, God will give you the strength to forgive each other.

Many couples married for forty or fifty years will tell you that forgiveness is essential in marriage. But how else do you work the muscle of forgiveness without confession? I was the first to confess since I had betrayed our vows, but Josh also had a sin he was hiding. When I led the way in sharing my sin, he followed and told me things he also had been hiding or struggling with. To this day, I expect him to share with me when he is thinking about or struggling with something alone. He has an accountability partner, but I also am a safe place to share if he has had anything distracting him from his relationship with God or me.

We want you to discover what we have—that sharing "something hard" will build a new, stronger marriage than you could ever dream of when you give your effort and allow God to do His supernatural work.

HONESTY BRINGS FREEDOM

The first instance of sin in marriage occurred in the garden of Eden. God provided the perfect union and circumstances, but we still find a man and woman sinning against God and each other. Do you remember Adam and Eve's response to their sins? They hid from God. They had been walking in communion with God daily, but after eating the forbidden fruit, they wanted to cover themselves with clothing and distance themselves from intimacy with their Creator because they felt embarrassed, sad, and guilty for what they had done. God immediately said to them, "Who told you that you were naked? Have you eaten of the tree of which I commanded you not to eat?" (Gen. 3:11 ESV). Basically, He was saying, "Who shamed you? Who is doing this to you? Because it's not Me." God wants you to stop being shamed and tormented by the Enemy.

It's a wild thought to me that God has seen and experienced every sin and struggle you have ever had—all your failures and shortcomings—and loves you unconditionally. This truth is hard to grasp because humans love so transactionally based on behavior. God's love is not like ours; His love is deeper than any pit we find ourselves in and greater than our biggest struggles. We are surrounded by oceans of His love just because we are His. When we grasp this truth, it gives us the courage to expose ourselves to one another. If God knows and sees all and still loves us, why would we try to hide from our spouse—whom He gave to us to become one with and walk together alongside Him?

If we want to have a new marriage, it starts with us confessing our sins to God and our spouse. Whether you have betrayed your vows and devastated your family, or your marriage is okay but still far from where you want it to be, now is the time to start. When you begin working your muscles of confession in small ways, we believe you and your spouse will see a supernatural work of unity.

I often think about some of my worst days before I confessed my sin to Josh. I remember the feeling of hiding and shame, knowing how far I had let my heart leave our home for another. When I look back, I picture myself standing at the foot of the cross, knowing the price Jesus paid for my sins. But every night I didn't confess was like another moment walking away from Jesus on the cross and saying no thanks. I didn't want to see the pain in His eyes, so I chose to keep fighting alone, believing the honesty required wouldn't be accepted, not realizing He had already paid the price for it.

Jesus has already paid for your forgiveness and peace; it is yours for the taking. But you must confess and repent first, accepting the love and price He paid on your behalf. His grace was too costly not to take it for yourself. Don't keep walking away from the cross and back into the shadows. Stay at the foot of the cross and receive healing that comes through confession.

Part Two

TAKE QUITTING OFF THE TABLE

ALLOW OTHERS TO BE A
PART OF YOUR STORY

YIELD TO VISION

You can quit on your marriage long before you leave. You may still be physically present, but are your heart and mind absent? Have you checked out mentally and spiritually? Are you just going through the motions? Part 2 is all about showing up and bringing your whole self to the solution. The marriage of your dreams is an all-in marriage, and there are no shortcuts to a wholehearted covenant.

53

Five

WHEN MY HEART
FEELS FAR AWAY

*Y*ou can have my feet," was the refrain I (Katie) said to the Lord repeatedly during the season when I desperately wanted out of our marriage. I meant that while my heart wasn't yet fully recommitted, my feet were, so I knew I wasn't going anywhere.

A dedication to not quitting reinforces the idea that you will remain physically present. Your feet are the most accessible place to start. Let your mind and heart follow. When women are in labor, there almost always comes the point when they don't believe they can go on. This is almost always right before they end up with a beautiful baby in their arms. When couples experience a crisis in their marriage, there is always a point when one or both people believe they can't go on. Similarly, it's almost always before a breakthrough. So if you're in the middle of a tough situation, I encourage you to give God your feet and keep moving forward in faith.

CULTIVATING A STRONG MARRIAGE

Is there any job that you feel positive you could not do? So many things come to mind for me here. I know many people can't imagine being in a room all day teaching either pre-schoolers or seniors in high school. Some may think they could never do physical labor, like bricklaying or landscaping. I have often thought about the discipline it takes to be a professional athlete, practicing the same skills repeatedly to perform them during a game or competitive event. But the one thing I feel certain I could never do is be a farmer. I can barely keep our fiddle-leaf figs alive, and I must confess we are "those people" who have returned them to Lowe's after trying multiple times.

On a serious note, statistics show that "farmers are among the most likely to die by suicide, compared with other occupations, according to a January [2020] study by the Centers for Disease Control and Prevention."[1] They believe the cause is stress from low-producing crops, isolation, and financial burdens, among other things.[2] I imagine it has a lot to do with endurance, too, when you think of their daily responsibilities. Preparing the land, planting seeds of hope, and then waiting for them to come to fruition without a guarantee. Tending to animals and protecting them from predators and disease. Early mornings; long, hot days; and late nights.

When you realize the attention, energy, and protection it takes to sustain this kind of life for you and your family, it's easy to make the jump in your mind from *husbandry*—the term used to describe the job of cultivating crops and caring for animals—to the term *husband*. Similar to the life of a farmer, marriage takes an enormous amount of endurance: trying every day to make the right choices, investing life-speaking words, confessing sins, forgiving wrongs, and loving as best you can . . . all with no guarantee that it will make a difference.

What happened with us six years into marriage actually came slowly and subtly. We had stopped doing the consistent work of preparing, planting, and caring for growth. We claimed marriage was a priority, but you wouldn't have seen that on our calendar, texts, daily talk time, weekly date nights, or getaways.

The endurance required when trying to out-serve each other in marriage every day is hard to maintain, even for couples in a healthy spot. But when you're going through a crisis or a hard season, it requires something supernatural to return to a place of health and growth. When I realized this simple truth, I knew I needed an extra measure of endurance to go all in with staying.

MOVING TO A NEW LAND

After my confession to Josh and the news of the affair becoming very public, the church in which he was pastoring asked him to step down. He was instructed to give his final sermon to the youth on a Wednesday night, and they asked me not to come to this service—or to ever walk back into the church again. We intended to keep living in our house as we worked to rebuild our marriage from the ashes, but it wasn't long before we realized how difficult this would be. Walking the same roads in our neighborhood where the other couple lived, driving the same streets, and working at a school under the judgmental eyes of so many parents was so hard, especially for a people pleaser who was more worried about everyone around me than the devastation in front of me.

We knew of a couple in Charleston, South Carolina, Mac and Cindy, whose marriage and family life we wanted to emulate. He was an incredible leader, and his wife adored him and their family. Plus, the health we saw in their teenagers and their church life was something we desperately wanted. My mom and stepdad had moved to Charleston several years earlier, and the city had always been a place we'd wanted to live. So we prayed, asking God for a way and a miracle, and put our house on the market.

The first person to get a job offer in Charleston was me, as a counselor at the juvenile detention center, so we asked God to show us whether He wanted us to move by getting us an offer on our house that day. After a long day of prayer and asking Him to show us His plan, our real estate agent called us at 10:00 p.m. with an offer to purchase our house. We fell to our knees because, after all we had been through, we knew this was a sign that God was still for us and was leading us to a new land, literally! Josh had a confident expectation that our marriage would go to a new land as well.

I was hopeful for our marriage but less sure than Josh at this point. I was still grieving the loss of what I considered love for another person, and I couldn't imagine rebuilding with Josh because my heart was so far gone. We have since met with many couples where one partner has felt similarly hopeless. Your marriage may not be suffering from the sin of infidelity, but maybe you are experiencing relational drift, which is still a far cry from the commitment you made to each other on your wedding day. No matter where you are right now, I encourage you to give Jesus your feet—to keep taking one step at a time as you follow His lead.

After three months in Charleston, Josh still hadn't found a job after applying everywhere, from insurance agencies to grocery stores. We were far from a sweet spot, but Josh was still faithfully holding out hope that better days were ahead. I didn't want to leave a man who loved me and was willing to do the work it took, but I honestly didn't want to do it.

I was so full of selfishness, self-doubt, and hopelessness, but I will never forget one particular Tuesday at 4:00 p.m. when I went out for a run. I began to run around the neighborhood we lived in and happened upon a track at an old high school down the road. I went in and ran around and around, just putting in the miles. I had worship music on in my ears, and I began to sob as I could see the time and energy it would take to rebuild. The daily, monotonous acts of denying myself, bringing my wounds to the Lord for healing, forgiving myself and Josh—the life-speaking words I would need to say.

That afternoon, running around and around that track with worship music playing, I realized for the first time that God would give me the strength to endure. On the walk home after that run, that's when I told the Lord, "You can have my feet." These were more than just words. They marked my commitment to endurance, even though I had no idea how to endure. I didn't know how else to grow the muscle of endurance except to endure—at least on my own. "You can have my feet" was a last-ditch effort to give it all to Jesus.

I wasn't giving Josh my feet. This was an integral distinction of my declaration. There was only One I could trust at this point. Josh had made his share of mistakes, had his share of impure motives, insecurities, anger, and doubts. He deserved my heart and feet, but I had already broken that bond of trust and needed to attach our hopes to something—no, *Someone*—more secure. Trusting Jesus became the most important part of our story because it was only Him who could bring about the new marriage we desperately needed.

LEARNING TO ENDURE

For us to not only endure the difficult seasons of marriage but create a brand-new relationship, we need to trust the Creator of every star in the sky, the fields that burst forth with life, and every creature under the sea and on the earth—including you and your spouse! Since God created us, He knows us better than anyone else knows us—including ourselves—and is capable of building in us the endurance needed to direct our feet to a place we could never get to on our own.

This path of staying, enduring, and hoping you can have a new marriage will require your head, hands, heart, and feet. It will require all of you, but I promise you don't need to have what it takes to start. You don't need fully developed muscles of endurance to begin to endure. He will walk with you, work with you, as you watch how He does it. The monotony of the days will start to turn. Building endurance was the most crucial element in bringing about a new marriage for us with the same person, and if I had chosen a different path, looking for shortcuts along the way, we would have missed the many promises and plans God had for us. That single act changed me and saved our marriage. I'm the furthest thing from a perfect wife, leader, mother, or friend, but I now recognize when I am beginning to leave instead of giving my feet to God and enduring along the path He lays out before me.

I don't know what past hurts you have brought into your marriage, but I know you have them. We all have wounds that need healing or scars to show what we've been through. By going to counseling and working on myself, I started to learn why I lacked some of the endurance I saw and admired in others. As a young girl watching my parents go through a divorce and seeing my dad move overseas six months later, I did not grow up with a model of enduring love. Throw in a lot of childish relationships based on what I thought was love by cultural standards, and you could say that instead of developing the muscle of endurance, I strengthened my ability to hide or escape anything that started to feel challenging.

No matter what your story is, I believe the Enemy's greatest temptation is for us to believe that Jesus is not trustworthy. That we can't count on Him. That He doesn't want what's best for us. That He will abandon us. But all of those are lies from the pit of hell.

Jesus never leaves.

Let that thought sink in. Even on your worst day, when you have run the farthest from Him, He will not leave you. He is never more than a breath away, watching, protecting, and wooing you with His love. He is close enough to count every hair on your head, and in His omniscience He can see the full story of your life and every promise and blessing coming for you. Will you trust Him to let the pages of your life unfold? Will you trust Him for provision, wisdom, revelation, and to do a new thing in your marriage? Will you give Him your feet? It's more than enough; He gave us His entire life and body. He has covered us, friends; let's endure and watch His unfailing love.

AN INVITATION TO A
NEWER, DEEPER LOVE

hen healing a marriage, it's important to move forward, not backward. This may seem obvious, but often couples try to "get back" to where they were before: the fluttery feeling of new love and excitement. The truth is, this may not be possible. More importantly, it's probably not the best thing anyway. During our rebuilding, I invited Katie not to return to an old place of pet names and puppy love but to a new, deeper place of intimacy. Something more stable, firm, and long-lasting.

Butterflies are great, but it's not what sustains a marriage. Marriages are meant to evolve and grow like the people in them, so we encourage you to trade in your false ideals of the past for the possibility of something better in the future.

Do you have any embarrassing nicknames from when you first started dating your spouse? What were they? I played sports, watched sports, and worked out a lot. All that to say, I was a guy, yet somehow names like *schnookie* and *sweet baby boo* seemed normal. I don't remember Katie and me calling each other any of these names, but we did write a lot of notes—where we'd call each other said names and profess our unmatched love for each other—and pass them in between classes or hide them in each other's cars. Katie would write in journals about me, processing her feelings and talking to God.

Did there ever come a point where you stopped calling each other those nicknames? A moment when the infatuation, daydreaming, and swoon of love seemed to fade, and you started calling each other by your actual names and talking like ordinary people? I don't remember when that happened for us, but it did. Within a couple of months of learning about the betrayal, there was a season where Katie and I were constantly traveling between Charleston and Columbia. Our home in Columbia was under contract when we moved, but it didn't work out. We had a rental, and Katie had a job in Charleston. We'd left the house in Columbia somewhat staged and regularly went back to pick up furniture, mow the yard, and keep the house maintained until it sold. On one visit, the kids had stayed in Charleston with Katie's parents, so it was just the two of us.

We were in that season of truth-telling and building trust through "confession therapy," which Katie already introduced. Whenever a thought came to mind—a memory, an emotion, something Katie had not confessed—she would share it with me. More often than not, as hard as it was to hear, her honesty gave me confidence in where she was mentally and emotionally. While I was sitting on the couch, which happened to be the only piece of furniture in the living room of that house in Columbia, Katie walked up with a stack of journals. I hadn't thought about schnookie, sweet baby boo, or any other names we'd called each other in years. That said, Katie opened one of the journals and pointed out a few of the nicknames. She had a question to ask and a statement to make. Her question was, "Do you still feel this way about me?" It was an interesting question because of the thoughts it brought to mind. Many of those nicknames were birthed in the hearts and minds of eighteen-year-old kids who had recently encountered the love of God and found love in their hearts for each other.

The first time I met Katie, which was a twenty-minute conversation in the lobby of the Patterson Hall dorm at the University of South Carolina, I went home afterward and told my roommate I was going to marry that girl. From that point on, she was everything I never knew I wanted. Sold out for God, beautiful, joyful, silly, and spontaneous. There was a lot about her I didn't know, yet somehow everything I knew I loved led me to believe I was willing to commit myself to her.

Forever. Seems crazy. We started dating about two months later, and it wasn't long until the nicknames began to flow. But back to the question, "Do you still feel this way about me?" I answered yes and no.

Yes, I still loved her so much that I was willing to sound and look stupid to communicate it. This season of brokenness in our marriage had shown me ways I'd allowed work and responsibility to get the best of me. Coming to the point of nearly losing her put everything in perspective. Positions, degrees, rental property, anything and everything without her were meaningless pursuits. Yes, I still felt this way about her.

My "no" was because of the type of love our nicknames represented. We were immature and had never experienced life's responsibilities, burdens, and distractions. We were in college, living on a meal plan, not a bill in the world— infatuated with each other. And, as happens with infatuation, our love was an intense but relatively short-lived passion and admiration for each other. But my love for her six years into our marriage was different; it was much more mature, grounded, and honest. Any sense of fantasy or fairy tale was gone. Instead of an emotional, seemingly involuntary obsession, my love for her now weighed the good and evil, the highs and lows, the "for better or worse" we'd once exchanged, and my choice was her. To love her in a way that felt much more meaningful.

That answered her question, but her statement was cut and dry. She said, "I don't feel this way about you anymore." Ouch. As a side note, if you ever find yourself in a season where your spouse's feelings have changed, that's okay. That may be one of the reasons you picked up this book. Don't let that scare you, don't become controlling, and don't try to fix it—because you can't. Feelings are fleeting; they are a good indicator but a lousy motivator. They tell *a* story but not *the* story. Jeremiah 17:9 says, "The heart is deceitful above all things and beyond cure. Who can understand it?" Isn't that the truth? Our hearts bring about feelings that become beliefs that shape our thoughts and inform our behaviors. All of which can seem so right yet be far from God's desire for our lives. He is sovereign over our emotions, has good in store for you, and wants your marriage to work.

This was one of many conversations where I felt just how powerless I was to fix our situation. I'd often find myself listening to Katie, begging God to give me the words to say. After hearing what she had to say, what came out of my mouth felt like an answer to prayer. God helped me to respond in a way that gave us vision and some new language to help us process what He wanted to do in our marriage. I said, "Katie, I'm not asking you to find your way back to an old place, to muster up feelings you once had. I'm inviting you to go to a new place, a deeper place of love."

Katie's question was pure; it wasn't a trick question, but it was not the best. Going back to the way we first felt about each other was not the goal. I'm not sure either one of us realized it until that moment. It was natural for us to desire what was easy, fun, and flirty. To visualize and want the times when we would laugh, enjoy each other, pursue each other, and make memories together. Let's return to that place; who doesn't want to go there? But, thankfully, the past was so broken that there was no going back. God wanted to do a new thing. He tried to take us to a new place. He wanted us to create a new marriage with the same person.

OUT WITH THE OLD

Generally speaking, I love the thought of new. I mean, who doesn't? New car, new clothes, new house—yes, yes, yes. Even the smell of new is exciting. When you open up a new pair of shoes, walk into a newly built home, or sit down in a new car, it's like the newness engages many of your senses; it looks, feels, and smells good. The tires aren't worn, there are no stains on the carpet or funk in the fridge, and even the bottoms of the shoes are clean. There are aspects of "new" that we all enjoy. However, there are times when "new" is painful, scary, and overwhelming.

Even though we may want new, we are comfortable with the old. We know how we got here; we remember what yesterday felt like, and because of that, we can anticipate tomorrow's experience to be similar. The old brings familiarity and predictability.

I've heard that change happens when the pain of staying the same is greater than the pain of changing.[1] When we are unhappy, discouraged, or frustrated, we can be confident that God is up to something. If we feel that way, it's only so that

He can get our attention long enough to allow Him to move and do a new thing. But just like Scripture says, we can't step into the unknown with a firm grip on the old: "Therefore, if anyone is in Christ, the new creation has come: The old has gone, the new is here!" (2 Cor. 5:17). We've got to let go of old thoughts, patterns, and behaviors to experience the new God has for us.

I remember when the good news about Jesus became personal for me. It was my junior year of high school, and I was at a youth event where an evangelist presented the gospel. I knew all about Jesus and could recite most of the familiar Bible stories, but this was the first time I sensed God speaking to me and inviting me to take a step, to get out of my seat and respond to Him. I was sitting in a row with some buddies I'd picked up on the way, and we were primarily there because it was night, girls were there, and I'd just started driving. Now, all of a sudden, tears were rolling down my cheeks, and God was doing something different. Something new. I felt the excitement and joy of hearing from God and experiencing His great love for me. The moment felt big; I knew it was real, it would change everything, and I wanted it.

On the other hand, I was scared to death. I played football, baseball, and basketball in high school, had many good friends and knew many great guys, none of whom seemed to be about Jesus and church. I still remember one of my friends asking, "What are you doing, bro?" as I started to cry and stood up that night. I didn't even know what to say; I had more questions than answers. But I knew I had to do it.

Though the old may bring familiarity and predictability, the new always requires faith and movement—faith that God is good and has good in store for you, and a willingness on your part to take a step. To move beyond what is to take hold of what could be. Ephesians 4:22–24 says it this way: "You were taught, with regard to your former way of life, to put off your old self, which is being corrupted by its deceitful desires; to be made new in the attitude of your minds; and to put on the new self, created to be like God in true righteousness and holiness."

The principle here is that the first step in experiencing a new marriage was allowing God to do new work in me. If you and I were to grab a cup of coffee and I asked you, "What new thing is God doing in your life?" what would you say? Are there ways He wants to use you? Truthfully, He wants to move from your head to your heart, from something you may know intellectually to something He is inviting you to feel or experience. Are there wounds He is working to heal or behaviors He wants you to do away with? It can be second nature for us to walk in the way of our old selves.

Choosing to be made new in our attitudes and deciding to put on the new self can't help but bring about newness in our marriage. Too often we focus on our problems instead of asking God, "What do You want to do in our marriage? What do You want to do in me?" God's way may be the longer road, and it may not bring about an immediate fix to what you are experiencing relationally, but I can assure you from experience that you will enjoy the new work God wants to do in your life and your relationship.

Matthew 9:17 best illustrates this. Jesus conversed with some of John the Baptist's disciples, saying, "Neither do people pour new wine into old wineskins. If they do, the skins will burst; the wine will run out and the wineskins will be ruined. No, they pour new wine into new wineskins, and both are preserved." Back then, animal skins were used for storing liquids, and fermented drinks, like wine, caused the skins to expand. Since old wineskins had already been stretched to their capacity, pouring new wine into them would cause the skin to rip and the wine and the wineskin to be ruined. Jesus made the point that He was there to do something completely new. To do new work in your marriage, Jesus has to do new work in you. Otherwise, you would be unable to sustain and enjoy the blessing He wants you to experience.

It's the difference between a good date and a great marriage. It's fairly easy to experience the former, but it takes commitment, time, and work to build the latter. Culturally, we see people short-circuit this process by building a new marriage with a new person. The only problem is that the new marriage is not made up of new individuals at all, but "old" people bringing with them their old thoughts, attitudes, and behaviors. What got them the results they experienced with their first spouse will be sure to surface with the next. When you take quitting off the table, when you start allowing God to do a new work in you, it sets the table for Him to bring about a new marriage with the same person. That's the kind of God He is and what the covenant is all about.

Isaiah 43:19 says, "See, I am doing a new thing! Now it springs up; do you not perceive it? I am making a way in the wilderness and streams in the wasteland." He is making a way, creating a path forward through what appears to be a dead end. He is bringing refreshment and life to places that may have felt dead and gone.

This was critical for Katie and me; it's why I'm so passionate about taking quitting off the table. Katie's heart was far gone, but she had told God she would not leave. Her physical presence and pursuit of God amid her struggle, plus my physical presence and pursuit of God in my pain, set the table for God to do a new thing.

What do you want to see God do in your marriage? Do you believe He wants you to have the life-giving, fun, flirty, and satisfying marriage you desire? Hebrews 11:6 says, "Without faith it is impossible to please God, because anyone who comes to him must believe that he exists and that he rewards those who earnestly seek him."

God is with you. God is for you. As you seek Him, be confident that He wants to bless you and bring about new life in you and your marriage.

Seven

NEXT RIGHT
ACTION

S o you're here and in it, committed to staying and not going anywhere. Now what? What next, and how do we walk forward taking the right actions every day when it feels like all we keep doing is failing each other?

I remember the day Josh and I moved to Charleston. We had put our dream house on the market to move into a small three-bedroom house we were renting, while trying to secure jobs and living on only 30 percent of what we were making previously. I don't know if you have moved before, but we are sadly very experienced in this, having moved fifteen times in our twenty years of marriage. I like to say we are the poor man's Joanna and Chip Gaines. When we moved to Charleston, our first home needed a total renovation—one that needed to happen in the hearts of its new renters.

When you first move into a house, it doesn't initially feel like it's yours. You may even question whether you made the right decision. *Does this house even feel like us, or will it ever?* The key to this transition time is taking the right steps daily. The first thing Josh and I do is move the furniture in and set up our beds; that way, when we tucker out and need to leave everything undone until the next day, the bed is ready. I'm pretty sure that's the top priority for you as well. The list that follows is based on your preferences, needs, wants, and what makes you feel at peace.

Some couples start with the kids' rooms, curating every detail and making them perfect, all while leaving their own room looking like a dumpster for months. Other couples may start in the kitchen or living spaces, prioritizing where they spend most of their time.

There is no right or wrong here because it's based on the two of you—your habits, lifestyle, and priorities. Well, there is actually a wrong—if you decide *not* to make a plan. Have you ever made a move or experienced a moment that you never intentionally discussed, only to find out later that you had entirely different pictures about what needed to happen next?

Josh and I have been there more times than we can count.

The night we got settled in Charleston and I went to bed in a house that was so much smaller than our last house—and in a town in which we had no community and Josh had no job—I lay in bed thinking, *What did we do? What are the next steps? How do we keep moving forward? Will all this be worth it?* I will never forget closing my eyes and thinking about all our children in the rooms next to us. Here we were in all our brokenness and pain, but we also felt a little free. We had nothing to prove because it seemed like all had been lost, so from this place, we would somehow start to rebuild.

Just like in a move, there will be priorities in your marriage that you will need to articulate to your spouse. What are the next right actions for you? Three key actions for Josh and me were to be open and honest, to have hard conversations, and to prioritize intimacy.

The key here is to keep taking steps. Outline the next right thing, talk about something you are hoping for, and watch God move mountains and do more than you could dream.

MOVE FORWARD WITH OPENNESS AND HONESTY

Josh and I focused on rebuilding our trust and intimacy. Anytime trust has been broken or shattered, you are left standing on a pile of rubble. Now, a pile of rubble may seem to most people a terrible place on which to rebuild, but it was the opposite for us. Actually, it would become the surest foundation we could have ever built on. Previously we had built our relationship on our ideal versions of each other, ones that suited our preferences. Any version of Josh that was not exactly ideal wouldn't do at all. And the same thoughts ran through Josh's mind about me. It was quite a disappointing blow to realize we were each uniquely imperfect. When standing on a pile of rubble, pretenses and ideal versions of each other are thrown out the window.

Have you and your spouse ever looked at each other and realized you are each staring at a broken and busted person? Have you seen the most unideal versions of each other, your shadow selves? You, in your sin. The way you are without the redeeming love of Jesus? None of us outgrows the cross or the need for a savior, and in this season of life where you are left shattered, you can easily admit it to yourself, your spouse, and most importantly, God.

When we began to outline the actions we needed from each other to rebuild trust, our list was short at first, but we needed to dedicate ourselves to the simplest form of love. Our first list of right actions involved honesty and openness. I gave Josh access to every device, text, and social media account, expecting him to monitor and check it to ensure accountability and integrity. Josh confessed his anger to the Lord, seeking healing from Him first, not me. During this season, we had to go down to one car, which made openness about our whereabouts much easier. To this day, though, we both have trackers on our phones and full openness with our locations.

SCHEDULE DIFFICULT CONVERSATIONS

The second thing we worked on was compartmentalizing our pain and heaviness, which may seem counterintuitive, but we did it not to escape the pain and hard work but to make sure we spent time focusing on good things. Both of us are people who enjoy life and seek to remain hopeful in all circumstances, but our lives had become overwhelmingly miserable. We had been to counselor after counselor in Columbia without many breakthroughs, and when we moved to Charleston just six months after I first confessed, we wondered how long our marriage would feel terrible. There was no quick three-step program anyone had offered us. No "say this, do that, and love will return." Thank God there wasn't because we never would have imagined how long it would feel in this season.

Looking back, though, we can't believe how short it was in the big picture, so we encourage you not to lose hope wherever you are right now.

Nonetheless, the road before us felt long. We found a great couple to mentor us, and they were willing to meet with us one night a week. We decided at this point to keep our heaviest conversations to these nights with them. Once we left them, we would stay up late talking about what they said and how it applied to us. Those nights were challenging before, during, and after we left their house, but we committed to staying in the hard conversations, and we had to work not to let them turn to fights because we knew we would lose the progress and momentum we were experiencing.

Having three small kids at the time, little money, and difficult day jobs, life was so heavy. We had moved to a city where we didn't have many friends, and we thought we had lost the calling of ministry, a job that filled us with purpose and joy.

You also have difficulties in life surrounding your marriage. Marriage is supposed to be a soft landing spot for life's harsh storms, not the most challenging part of life. But when it is—and it will be if you stay long enough—the best thing we learned to do during this time was to compartmentalize the heaviness and pain as much as we possibly could.

For us, this looked like me getting off work on a Tuesday night and coming home to snacks Josh had prepared and a glass of wine sitting out. We would walk the kids down to the park and work to enjoy them. I often got the kids down for bed and then we would each watch our own show or would read our books near each other until we got in bed together. Some would say doing life side by side does not build intimacy, but we would disagree. Finding ways to get outside together, lighten the day, or laugh together is needed and is good medicine for hard times. But in order to keep moving forward in building your new marriage, you cannot plan and enjoy the fun times without scheduling the difficult conversations and committing to being fully engaged in them. We suggest reading this book and choosing a couple who will walk through it with you once a week. If you can't find a couple who will commit to this, then sit down together weekly to talk through each chapter together. On the other days, do the right actions to build the intimacy your covenant needs.

PRIORITIZE PHYSICAL INTIMACY

The last area we focused on during this time was physical intimacy. This was especially vital for Josh because it is his love language, and for him to feel secure in my love, he needed to know that this was a priority for us. I committed to a weekly rhythm that we decided on together and sought to serve him and our covenant in this way until I was feeling any emotions sexually. I'm including this piece in here because sex is the most complicated but essential issue most couples face. It's the one thing that distinguishes you as a married couple from being just friends or roommates. Your sexual intimacy is a God-given gift designed to bring unity in your marriage. During the act, we know from science, but moreover biblically, that you are joining together physically, mentally, emotionally, and spiritually.

In a season of betrayal, heartbreak, lost love, pain, and grief, this one principle done as unto God can bring more healing than you can imagine.

TURN BREAKTHROUGHS
INTO HEALTHY HABITS

Every person, relationship, and set of issues is different, so our three first actions that I just discussed may not be what you need.

You and your spouse need to determine what first steps you need to begin taking every day, and then go all in on those. Whether you are recognizing patterns that could lead you down the wrong path, or you are so deep in the woods that you cannot see a way out—you will want to commit to those first steps regardless of the immediate changes you may or may not be experiencing. Josh and I started to get breakthroughs in different areas at different times, and it likely will be no different for you. Sometimes it can feel like two steps forward and three steps back, but the truth is, you are growing in some areas, which often highlights weaknesses in other areas. Keep going back to actions you can take that will begin to form habits you can build a healthy, new marriage on.

The book *Atomic Habits* is one of our all-time favorites, and we would recommend reading this if you haven't. After reading this work by James Clear, as well as hearing him speak on podcasts, I came to the conclusion that once we determine the *what*, then we are able to form a daily habit or routinely follow an action plan to promote this path of intimacy and keep cultivating it.

Talk through the following questions with your spouse to help you map out the actions needed to rebuild your covenant.

1. What feels most shattered and hopeless?
2. What makes us feel most fruitful and happy as a couple? (Describe the seasons, days, and moments we feel most alive.)
3. What do we need to do to protect our answers for number 2, individually and as a couple?
4. What is one simple step we can take this week to let each other know we are committed to moving in the right direction?

Josh and I decided that we—only the two of us—needed to start regularly sharing about our days, and not just about the heart-heavy topics but everything and anything, to cultivate a friendship. We encourage you to do the same. Commit to calling and texting each other *first* with good or bad news, instead of after you've told someone else. When you think of a great story, see a funny video, or hear a hilarious joke, send it to your spouse. Watch shows together. Find things you like to do together outside. Building these habits is what a friendship and beautiful life are built on, and it's amazing how often and easily we neglect them.

MOVE FROM ONE RIGHT ACTION TO THE NEXT

Once you choose the new habit you want to build, give yourself a trigger point to practice the habit daily. You will want to work on one new habit at a time.

Here is an example: I want to speak words of life, love, and encouragement over my husband.

Trigger: When he finishes getting dressed in the morning and is about to leave for work.

Habit: Speak life over him before he leaves. "You look so good!" "I am praying for you today." "I am thankful for . . ."

Reward: Give yourself a reward every time you do it.

Make it small and healthy so it's a win-win! Journal it, give yourself a check mark, and then at the end of the week, get a small treat.

Habit building is simple, but most people don't do it because they are not willing to put in the daily, consistent work needed. You can do this! And please know that you are not in this alone. Far from it. When I think about this season of our marriage—when it was right actions, right movement, but not seeing miracles immediately—I think about the story of Ruth in the Bible.

When the story opens, Naomi's sons had just died. She was deeply grieving and asked her two widowed daughters-in-law to call her Mara, meaning "bitter." Josh and I both resonate with this place of deep loss and sadness. In the Bible story, Naomi urged Ruth and Orpah to remain in Moab with their paternal families and to leave her. Orpah agreed, but Ruth, in an act of unusual faithfulness, stayed with Naomi and traveled with her. There was no security, no assurance that they would be provided for, victorious, or happy. Ruth just chose to do the next right thing and be faithful, just as God had been faithful to her.

> "Wherever you go, I will go; and wherever you lodge, I will lodge; your people shall be my people, and your God, my God. Where you die, I will die, and there will I be buried. The Lord do so to me, and more also, if anything but death parts you and me." (Ruth 1:16–17 NKJV)

Together they journeyed to Naomi's former home in Bethlehem, where they learned they would have to provide for themselves. They went to work; nothing was being handed to them, and they knew there was a long road ahead. When it was time for the barley harvest, Ruth decided to glean from a field.

Next right action.

Although she didn't know it, the field she chose belonged to Boaz, a wealthy kinsman of Naomi's family. When Boaz visited the field and heard of Ruth's loyalty to Naomi, he instructed his workers to allow her to glean undisturbed and even to leave additional grain in her path. Meanwhile, Naomi was trying to find a husband for Ruth, so she asked her to go to the threshing floor on the night Boaz winnowed barley. She instructed her to wash and prepare herself, uncover Boaz's feet, and lie next to them while he slept.

Next right action.

This Ruth did. When Boaz awoke, startled to find Ruth at his feet, she asked him to spread his robe over her—a symbolic act of choosing him as her husband—because Boaz was a "redeemer" (Ruth 3:12 esv). In biblical times, it was his right to redeem the property of a family member who had died and to also marry the widow. Boaz was amazed by Ruth's faithfulness, and they eventually married.

Next right action.

Here is the wild truth for you: the next right actions lead to actual miracles. This was true for Josh and me. I could write ten books telling you about all God did for us that year while we were rebuilding out of the rubble of our marriage, our desire for each other, and our dreams. As you move forward guided by God, He will move mountains and perform miracles in your lives and marriage that will astound you, just as He did for Ruth. She and Boaz went on to have a son named Obed, who was father to Jesse, who was the father of King David. When you read the honored lineage of our Savior, you will read about Ruth and Boaz.

Our stories are not our own; they are a part of a greater story. I promise that's why the Enemy wants yours. He knows that if he can stop you, he can stop the plans of Jesus coming into the lives of others through you. When we are faithful to take the right actions, God will bring about breakthroughs and miracles far beyond our greatest hopes and wildest dreams.

Part Three

*H*ealing a marriage is very hard to do alone. You need encouragement, accountability, and examples of people who have been through something similar and come out the other side. This means trusting the right people, in the right ways, at the right time.

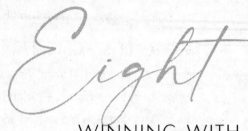

WINNING WITH COMMUNITY

Katie loves going to the beach. If we've got a free evening or an open Saturday, her first recommendation is always, "Let's go to the beach." Now, don't get me wrong; I love the beach. It's beautiful. The sunrise, the sunsets, the breeze, the water. I just don't love the idea of going to the beach with our whole family. There are nine of us, with our kids currently ranging in age from toddler to twenty. Some love the vibe and could hang out for hours; others start asking what time we are going home shortly after arriving. All the towels and toys, boards and balls, food and drinks . . . and plus, it's not that enjoyable being the mule carrying everything from the car and then back again a few hours later. And don't get me started about all the sand that ends up filling the car! It's so much work. Yay. Let's go to the beach.

In the fall of 2022, Katie and I thought it was time to start a small group, something we hadn't done in a while. We had recently met a lot of couples who were new to the area or just in a new season and didn't feel like they were connected or had a sense of community. Now that we had finished writing this book, our schedules were more open, and we thought it was time. Since mamas primarily run the house, Katie started texting the ladies on details. What night, where to meet, who brings what, and other logistics. After a week or two of texting, talking, and planning, Katie told me one Saturday that we would be meeting the next night for the first time. "Good stuff!" I said. "Where?" The last I'd heard, we planned to alternate homes so that it wasn't too much burden on anyone. But I'm sure you've already guessed her response: "The beach." What? Am I being punked right now? She put me on the hook for a weekly small group, family dinner beach trip.

The next day came and we transported all of our kids and stuff, got out to the beach, and got everything set up. As usual, it was a lot. While we talked with friends, another family with seven kids arrived, but in addition to the large-family beach gear, the dad also had a guitar and a drum! This made me thankful I'm not very musical! Katie loves the idea of family worship, all of us singing together, going after God.

Something that I would love if I weren't constantly counting kids because I'm worried about someone getting lost or eaten. But within about fifteen minutes, our kids were laughing, making friends, and playing together, and we adults were processing where and how we need to grow in our marriages and what we hoped to see God do. After a little while, my buddy started playing the guitar, and half the kids joined us in worshiping while we could hear the others running around and laughing in the background. About that time the sun began to set and I found myself thinking, *There is nowhere else on earth I would rather be.* We were connecting with friends and experiencing God's presence, which we were modeling for our kids. It was beautiful. And I'm so glad I overcame my resistance to meeting at the beach so I could experience that moment.

RESISTANCE BUILDS STRENGTH

Where in your life do you experience resistance? A delay, hesitation, or maybe an outright refusal to do something that will ultimately be good for you? Possibly it's in regard to the food you eat. Katie wants me to be gluten-free so bad. One of our daughters is, and it has resolved all her stomach issues; her skin glows, and she looks healthy. Or it could be related to fitness. You want to start exercising, running, jogging, biking, or going to the gym. You've gotten out a time or two and would like to make it a habit, but the demands of the day keep you busy, make you tired, and seem to war against making any real change. Resistance rises from within and you reason away any motivation to move toward your goal. We've all been there at one point and have different ways of experiencing it.

One area of resistance most people share in some capacity is regarding community. One survey found that roughly 52 percent of Americans consider themselves to be introverted,[1] so those people need time alone with their thoughts, ideas, and feelings to feel refreshed, and they'd rather hang out with just one or two people, which makes them naturally resistant to the idea of spending time with a group of people. But whether you are introverted or extroverted, our lives are often at capacity: work, school, kids, home, bills, extended family, birthdays, holidays, sports—the list goes on and on. Often, we can hit the end of the day or the end of the week having successfully accomplished everything we *had* to do but find ourselves dreaming of doing the things we *want* to do. Putting something else on the calendar, deciding to orient your life around a group of people to process God's Word, your life, or how the two of them come together, is one more thing you feel you just don't have time for.

Now think of those seasons when you are hurting in your marriage. Maybe like the one you're in right now. You're feeling beat down and discouraged, things are complicated and difficult, and so the last thing you want is to be around others. But the fact that your cup is half-empty and you feel as though you are regularly in need of encouragement, direction, or counsel to be filled up is the exact reason why you need community.

Part of the reason Katie and I ended up in the situation we did was because we had lost our community. The same is true for many of the couples we have counseled. When you sense that your marriage is beginning to suffer, look around and you'll almost certainly realize you are fighting your battles on your own. And that's just where Satan wants you to be—alone, isolated, and without any encouragement from a community of believers.

CHOOSE ALLIES WISELY

When we moved to Charleston, we knew we needed godly people in our lives to speak truth to us and to help us be accountable in our marriage. We weren't ready to handle conflict alone yet, so that is why we sought out a Christian couple to mentor us. Katie mentioned them in the last chapter, and during our time with them each week, we were able to bring our arguments and issues to these friends, who helped us navigate our difficult path toward wholeness. The man spurred me on to becoming a godly husband, and the woman held Katie's face and spoke truth to her over and over again.

We didn't choose a couple haphazardly; rather, we prayed, observed people in our church, and had conversations with couples almost as if we were interviewing them. If you don't already have people in your lives who can speak truth into your marriage, challenge you to love and honor your spouse, and hold you accountable, we encourage you to find them now—whether your marriage is in a great place or on shaky ground.

God desires healing and wholeness for you. He wants you to be fully alive and satisfied in your marriage. There are places of friendship, intimacy, joy, and delight that will be experienced only through covenant with another. Likewise, there are breakthroughs, healing, learning, and growth that happen in a community with others. Hebrews 10:24–25 reads, "Let us consider how we may spur one another on toward love and good deeds, not giving up meeting together, as some are in the habit of doing, but encouraging one another." Do you need to experience new measures of grace? Do you need healing for places of pain? Perhaps the best next step you can take is toward community. It is when we confess our sins "one to another," when we humble ourselves among trusted friends to share our places of struggle and shame, that God brings about healing. Sin isolates us; even in our pain, our pride can keep us from sharing the truth of our story. But James 4:6 tells us, "God opposes the proud but gives grace to the humble" (ESV).

TRUE FRIENDS STAY WITH YOU IN THE MESS

I've always felt this pressure to have the answers, to be successful, to know what I'm doing. However, anyone who has ever stepped into a new job, marriage, or done anything of significance will tell you there are going to be times when you don't have the answers, where you feel like a loser and have no clue what you are doing. When that happens in your vocation, there are so many options since it's unlikely you're the first person to walk through whatever you are experiencing. Grab a book, listen to a podcast, and seek counsel. None of these is a sure fix, but at least there are steps you can take. But when you face difficulty in your marriage, it can often seem as though no one has ever experienced what you're going through and that there is no escaping it.

Home is supposed to be our one area of refuge. The place to which we can retreat to find rest and refreshment. I'd always thought life at home was supposed to be easy. Natural. But when home life feels like hard work and *you* are part of the problem, it's even more challenging to seek counsel and get help. So Katie and I didn't. And maybe that's your story too. We kept working on our marriage as best we knew how, and I mistakenly confused work with progress. It wasn't until I heard Katie say, "I don't know if I love you anymore" that all bets were off and I acknowledged that our future didn't look promising. My attempts at working on us had helped get us there, and now I understood how desperately we needed help from godly men and women who would give us a fresh perspective, pray for us, and walk with us.

Katie's mom, Debbie, had long been sending me CDs and DVDs of a guy named Mac Lake. At the time, he was the leadership development pastor at Seacoast Church, so amid the mess, I called to schedule an appointment with him in Charleston. I always wanted to be a good husband, father, and pastor, but truth be told, I had no vision of what that trifecta of goodness was supposed to look like. Until I met Mac. I don't remember anything about our conversation other than coming away realizing he embodied what I wanted to be. He loved God, was passionate about his wife, had a fantastic family, and was crushing it in ministry. So I asked him, "Can I wash your car, cut your grass, do anything to be around you?" He laughed and said, "Yes. Cindy and I have felt called to start a married couples small group. You and Katie could join it!"

Within a couple of weeks, we joined their Friday night group. Being unemployed and broken, I wasn't posturing for anybody. No need to pretend I was successful; other than our children, there wasn't anything I could point to at this time to take pride in. I'd been fired from my job, and my wife didn't love me anymore. All I had was faith that God could bring healing, and I trusted Him to use this group and space to do it. Although we now know some great Christian marriage counselors in our area, at the time we struggled to find the right one, so we had to rely on other Christian couples to encourage and guide us.

At first, the small group included five to six couples, but about a month later every other couple had dropped out for various reasons—shift changes, family dynamics, all sorts of things. It ended up being Mac, Cindy, Katie, and me every Friday night for the next three or four months.

There was something about being with Mac and Cindy. Although they'd never experienced anything like what Katie and I were walking through, nor were they licensed counselors, they loved God and His Word, and they knew what He could do in our lives and marriage. We'd bring the conversations that would lead to a fight at home to their living room, which became a place of peace. A house of miracles. Sharing our greatest pain, fears, insecurities, needs, and sin with them opened the door for God to bring about healing. They were a neutral, faith-filled voice that wasn't fighting for Josh or Katie but Josh *and* Katie.

Now whenever Katie and I sit with couples in a hard spot, my concern for them isn't about *what* but *who*. In time, God is faithful to surface every thought, belief, attitude, or behavior that needs to start or stop, but that isn't nearly as important as who you are in Christ. Who in your life is walking with you, or you feel confident would walk with you, through the messiest of times? You don't walk anywhere fast. It takes consistency, time, and faithfulness. Who in your life loves God and embodies what you want for your marriage? Someone who loves you but isn't all that impressed with you. Who is willing to listen, love, and say the hard things. But most of all, who is willing to walk with you. They are showing up and sharing. Because God did the impossible in us, I'm confident He can do anything in you.

Meeting with Mac and Cindy rewired some things in Katie and me, and once God had restored our marriage, some new tools were in our toolbox. When Katie and I came to an impasse in a heated conversation, we now knew that we could grow faster and move further ahead by "fighting with friends" instead of "fighting alone." For example, one night, while Katie and I were on a date, I remember getting into an argument and feeling stuck, so we called our friends Josh and Lisa, who were also out on a date, and asked if we could meet up. We sat outside a Starbucks and talked about what happened and how we felt. I have no clue what the issue was, but I remember talking, laughing, praying, and heading home to end date night the right way!

Inviting friends into our fights has become a discipline for us. It's embarrassing and requires humility, but it always brings breakthroughs. Now, don't let this be the only reason you get together with these trusted friends, and we suggest you ask ahead of time whether they would be comfortable taking part in such discussions. And to further strengthen your community of friends, let them know you are available and willing to help them in the same manner.

MOMENTARY STRUGGLES LEAD TO FUTURE VICTORIES

If we were to sit down and talk about your life and start to process your relationships, work, health, thoughts, and faith, what areas of struggle would surface? We all ride the struggle bus on occasion. Struggle or strain is a natural response to resistance. To the challenges and opposition of life. One thing about struggling is that the closer you are to the source of opposition, the harder it is to see clearly. It can be hard to see the big picture because we are so focused on the details that most impact us in the moment.

And when you add to the mix other everyday life struggles—adjusting to a newborn, navigating life with a teenager, dealing with a car repair, appeasing a demanding boss, and so much more—they only compound your marital difficulties. Sometimes we see and are willing to discuss our struggles; other times we have our heads down, grinding, working hard, getting through the day. It can take someone else looking at our life from the outside to say, "What are you doing?!" A great example of this is found in Exodus 18:13–24:

The next day Moses took his seat to serve as judge for the people, and they stood around him from morning till evening. When his father-in-law saw all that Moses was doing for the people, he said, "What is this you are doing for the people? Why do you alone sit as a judge, while all these people stand around you from morning till evening?" Moses answered him, "Because the people come to me to seek God's will. Whenever they have a dispute, it is brought to me, and I decide between the parties and inform them of God's decrees and instructions." Moses' father-in-law replied, "What you are doing is not good. You and these people who come to you will only wear yourselves out. The work is too heavy for you; you cannot handle it alone. Listen now to me and I will give you some advice, and may God be with you. You must be the people's representative before God and bring their disputes to him. Teach them his decrees and instructions, and show them the way they are to live and how they are to behave. But select capable men from all the people—men who fear God, trustworthy men who hate dishonest gain—and appoint them as officials over thousands, hundreds, fifties and tens. Have them serve as judges for the people at all times, but have them bring every difficult case to you; the simple cases they can decide themselves. That will make your load lighter, because they will share it with you. If you do this and God so commands, you will be able to stand the strain, and all these people will go home satisfied." Moses listened to his father-in-law and did everything he said.

Now, we all expect to struggle in our twenties, thirties, and forties. We tell ourselves lies to keep us moving forward: that we're smart enough, have learned enough, or have earned enough to resolve our struggles, to ease the strain. That we'll figure this out at some point. Moses was God's man, whom He chose to lead the children of Israel out of captivity. Moses had seen God do amazing things both in and through him. Yet here he was, around the age of eighty, riding the struggle bus when it came to his everyday job. From sunup to sundown, he worked as hard as he could to serve and care for people, all the while neglecting his family and wearing himself out. It took someone with a relationship, proximity, and consistent presence in his life to say, "Moses, what are you doing?"

Who in your life is close enough and courageous enough—and to whom you've given permission—to say, "What are you doing?" Do you have people or couples who care enough about you to point out the shortcomings and sins and blind spots that you can't see? If you have friends who can call you out and call you up to a higher level, that's great. The bigger question is, are you willing to take their counsel?

Proverbs 27:17 says, "As iron sharpens iron, so one person sharpens another." I researched that process and learned that if one of the irons has a different texture, the iron could be sharpened even better and faster than if the blades were the same. Likewise, when you bring two people together with diverse backgrounds, experiences, and perspectives to walk alongside each other and build a relationship, the sharpening will happen better and faster.

For example, in our small group last week, one guy shared that he was concerned about the integrity of his family. He's realized that they say they will start or stop something, but the next day they are back where they started. Upon sharing this struggle, another guy spoke up and said, "Bro, you have two kids under two. Your kids are still up during the night, taking naps throughout the day; this is a difficult season of life to make plans. This season is all about making and changing plans." When concerns and struggles walk with wisdom and experience, strengthening happens.

A TRIBE IN TIMES OF TROUBLE

Trouble is a promised reality in all our lives. Jesus said, "In this world you will have trouble" (John 16:33). If and when it surfaces, it's important to remember the second half of that verse: "But take heart! I have overcome the world." He is with you, and in Him, you are never alone when in trouble. That's good news for all of us.

There will be times when you bring the trouble on yourself, maybe by giving in to a sin, making a poor decision, or hanging around the wrong people. Other times trouble will find you—when something beyond your control knocks you down and leaves you questioning if or how you will get through it. Ecclesiastes 4:9–10 says, "Two are better than one, because they have a good return for their labor: If either of them falls down, one can help the other up. But pity anyone who falls and has no one to help them up."

The best time to find community and build a tribe is before you're in desperate need of one. When you find yourself in trouble, regardless of how you got there, if you are connected and living in a community, your tribe will find you. They come after you.

Genesis 14 tells the story of Abram's nephew Lot, who had chosen to separate himself and his family geographically and spiritually from the community of God. In doing so, Lot settled near Sodom and Gomorrah. There came the point where four kings had allied themselves with one another and raided Sodom and Gomorrah, carrying off all its goods and many of its people, including Lot and his possessions. Then this happened:

> When Abram heard that his relative had been taken captive, he called out the 318 trained men born in his household and went in pursuit as far as Dan. During the

night Abram divided his men to attack them and he routed them, pursuing them as far as Hobah, north of Damascus. He recovered all the goods and brought back his relative Lot and his possessions, together with the women and the other people. (vv. 14–16)

A couple of important things to note here. Lot had primarily brought this on himself because of where he'd chosen to live. Sodom and Gomorrah were dark places. But that didn't keep Abram from going to fight for Lot. The house of Abram had a culture that was supposed to resemble the culture of God's church. By living in community and identifying yourself as a follower of Christ, you are not only a friend but a brother or sister in Christ, and when you find yourself in trouble, watch out, because Christ's community rolls deep, and we will come for you.

I've got countless examples of how our church community has shown up as our tribe. The week of Christmas in 2008, after two full days of loading the U-Haul and then driving to our new home, I was surprised to find a crowd of men waiting to help unload the truck when I arrived in Charleston at 8:00 p.m. My father-in-law's men's group at his church rallied to show us this would be the kind of place where people show up for you.

After we got settled into the rental, the sale of our home in Columbia fell through. I was still unemployed, trying to pick up odd jobs, and things were getting tight financially. I heard about our church's Acts 4 Family Fund, where people at the church give above and beyond their tithe so that the church can help support people in a tight spot. I met with a pastor, and the church helped cover some of our bills for several months until we got on our feet. It showed us that this was the kind of community where people show up in times of need.

God positions his people in this place and time for a purpose. Acts 17:26 says this: "From one man he made all the nations, that they should inhabit the whole earth; and he marked out their appointed times in history and the boundaries of their lands." That means God has been very intentional about your when and where. Of all the times in history and all the places in the world, He chose this place and this time for you. When we plant ourselves in a local church and get involved in building community, it's so that we might commit ourselves to one another as brothers and sisters in Christ.

PROVISION IN THE MIDST OF PAIN

When was the last time you experienced pain? It may have been emotional rather than physical pain. Perhaps the loss of a loved one. An unexpected separation that has left you devastated. I've been walking with a friend recently who experienced that. He called one day and asked about any small groups of men who don't want to give up, who want to grow and fight for their marriage. I called our church's small groups pastor and told him about his situation. Our pastor said, "I've got the perfect group." I started a text thread introducing my friend to Mark, the group's leader, who immediately met with him since it was a holiday weekend and the group wouldn't be meeting for a couple of weeks. Mark didn't know this dude, but he had compassion for him and knew that he could bring about provision by way of his presence.

Second Corinthians 1:3–4 says, "Praise be to the God and Father of our Lord Jesus Christ, the Father of compassion and the God of all comfort, who comforts us in all our troubles, so that we can comfort those in any trouble with the comfort we ourselves receive from God." Those times when we are in trouble, we need a tribe to fight on our behalf and to extend compassion, comfort, and support to us. It's in those moments when we feel alone and in distress that God uses our community, our church family, to be the source of provision for our pain.

There are several pastors around the country whom I listen to regularly, one of whom is Craig Groeschel. I've heard him say, "What if the greatest enemy to the life that you want is the life that you are living?"[2] We all know the value of community and meaningful relationships, so why do we so often try to live without them? I was a pastor, working in a church, surrounded by people, yet Katie and I were largely isolated. No one knew the struggles and brokenness we were experiencing in our marriage. Thankfully, we finally allowed God to use a group of people to walk with us and help bring healing and breakthrough. If you surround yourself with a godly community that is willing to walk by your side through your worst days and never stop fighting for you, you will step into the life and marriage you've always wanted.

Nine

JESUS IS KINDER
THAN ANY CHRISTIAN
YOU KNOW

The day after I confessed my affair, Josh went into the church that we loved so he could meet with and tell the lead pastor. He was already aware since he had received a late-night call from the parents of the other couple involved, who were elders in the church. It wasn't my meeting, and looking back, I'm still not sure how much Josh was protecting me; he knew I was already feeling an overwhelming amount of shame, but I honestly had no clue where we went from here and what would be the result of this meeting.

The whole time he was gone, my mind was racing because I knew the outcome of the meeting would mark out our path forward. Would there be forgiveness and rehabilitation for our marriage? Would they ask Josh to leave for a time and help us rebuild? Could we rebuild? Would we continue as if nothing had happened? If so, then I would have had to walk into church pretending that words and emotions had not been shared with another man, breaking my vows and my husband's trust.

When Josh got home around eleven that morning, I met him at the door to hear the news. "They asked me to preach my last message to the youth group this Wednesday night, not sharing any details, and to tell the students I was leaving."

"They asked that you not come back to the church?"

That was all he said.

Never having been in this kind of situation before, I guess I didn't know to expect any different. Our path was laid out quickly and clearly. We were on our own.

The next night, Josh and I drove over to his parents' home because he wanted his mom and dad to hear the story from me first and not from other people, as conversations and rumors were already spreading quickly. People were creating their own stories without knowing the details, and Josh knew we would not be able to spend energy mitigating gossip if we wanted to save our marriage.

While we drove in silence, all I could think of was the look of disappointment I would see on Josh's dad's face. I didn't know what he or my mother-in-law would say, but I knew their eyes would say more than their words; the eyes are what I feared the most. Josh's dad was a hero to me, so telling him and Josh's mom was one of the hardest things I have ever done. They had every right to be upset, to show their disappointment with their words or expression, but instead they had such love and compassion for me, and it was the first time since confessing to Josh that I saw a glance of kindness my way. We asked them what we should do next, and they didn't know either. I had a job at a school, and the church was paying Josh a couple of weeks' severance. And so we knew, at least for now, Josh needed to start looking for a job and we needed to find a counselor.

CONVICTION VERSUS CONDEMNATION

The weeks and months that followed were some of the worst of my life. I wouldn't wish the pain of my shame and the judgment of others on anyone. If you have confessed something in your marriage that broke your vows and devastated the trust you had built over the years, you may understand some of what I am saying. If you have never reached this point, I hope you never do—and hopefully our story will be warning enough to repair the minor things before they become catastrophes.

Conviction by the Holy Spirit is good and will lead us to change and healing. However, shame and condemnation are crafted and used by the Enemy to kill, steal, and destroy.

It's as old as the garden of Eden. When you fall short in any area, the Enemy wants you to hide from God. This is why the biblical confession we discussed in the confession therapy chapter is so powerful in marriage. Hiding and keeping secrets make you run first from yourself, then from your spouse, friends, and even God. Shame does the same thing. Beyond the Holy Spirit's conviction, once you start feeling the judgment of others and believing the lies the Enemy is telling you about who you are, you are in shame territory, making you feel unloved and unworthy. This quickly progresses to hopelessness, and hopelessness is the train track to death. Death of purpose, love, vision, dreams, confidence, security, contentment, trust, and ultimately your marriage covenant.

In the weeks and months post-confession, I battled shame hourly and grew so weary trying to fight the lie that what I had done was so deeply wrong that my brokenness was irreparable. I became so scared of myself and how capable I was of sinning and of hurting others—even God. I was sure I was unlovable to God, unusable to Him, and would never have the close relationship with Him that I used to lean on. It seemed all my relationships were shattered at this moment, because everyone I loved and trusted was deeply disappointed in me. I had no interest in working to rebuild their trust while trying to rebuild with Josh.

Some people would try to make me feel better by telling me more lies, such as "What you did isn't that bad" or "You deserve to be happy" or "You should do what you want to do." Deep down, though, I knew none of these things would change how I felt, because even if I walked out of my marriage, I would be taking myself with me. I was in no position to know what I wanted or needed. From this place of loneliness and isolation, the Enemy of my soul started to have a field day, and I couldn't remember ever feeling that low.

Before we moved to Charleston, we drove down to visit a church in North Charleston called the Seacoast Dream Center. We hadn't been going to church regularly since the confession three months prior because it was hard to find a safe space in our community where we were not known and judged, at least in my mind. One evening while in Charleston, we spent time with my parents at their home, and after dinner, Josh stepped outside to take a phone call. When he came in, he told me we needed to go for a walk and talk.

The call was from the other couple involved, and the woman told him a detail I had not yet confessed to Josh. We were working to rebuild trust by me telling him everything, so withholding this information was a blatant betrayal. It would take almost another year for me to disclose more and more until I fully opened up to Josh about everything.

In the first six months following my confession, I also found a way to contact the other man, and I would reach out, wanting not to feel like such a monster or hoping that what I felt for him and from him was love. I reached out to him while assuring myself it was harmless because neither one of us was going to leave our marriage. I share this because we have walked with so many couples who confessed or caught their partner in the act of betrayal, and it has taken months or years to free themselves from the sin. Maybe you're not meeting with another person physically, but you are still doing so on an emotional level. I want you to know you are not alone. We are not bulletproof, and when you are in a low season and allow the Enemy to creep into your life, you can be weaker than you ever dreamed.

I want to say so clearly, though, that until all ties are broken and you are truly walking in freedom, there is no way to start to rebuild your marriage and see all God can do. I never imagined in those months following our affair that we would see God shift in the coming years and change us as quickly and powerfully as He did. He is more invested in your freedom from shame, the Enemy's hold, addiction, and self-hate than you are.

I was still stumbling along the way at this point, and after that phone call when Josh learned of another betrayal I had kept hidden, he was devastated. He told me that he could not sleep in bed with me that night and would need to sleep on my parents' couch. You can imagine my parents were devastated, too, and they must have felt helpless watching two people they loved go through this. My mom had been through a divorce herself, and she knew full well the pain that it still carried over twenty years later. And because I had lived through her divorce as a child, I had a glimpse of what my kids would walk through if Josh and I severed our relationship. If there is any hope in having a new marriage with the same person, there is so much reason to endure the pain.

That night, hopelessness had finally taken root and I felt

that I couldn't move forward. I didn't see any way to repair my relationship with Josh and regain his complete trust. I also couldn't see a way forward with myself. I knew God must be disappointed beyond measure and was sure He didn't want anything to do with me. I will spare you the details in order to not let the Enemy occupy space in anyone else's mind, but I came so close to ending my life that night because my thoughts of self-hate were starting to overpower my will to live.* In my darkest moment, I glanced at my Bible on the nightstand and grabbed it. As I desperately held on to it, something happened that changed my life forever.

I heard God's voice.

Not an audible voice in the room but so loud and clear in my spirit that I knew it was my heavenly Father.

He said, *Katherine, I love you. I have plans for your life. I knew this day would come when I created you, and I love you.*

That was it. That simple but powerful message changed me forever. I had not heard those words from anyone in the weeks and months prior.

I learned then that Jesus was kinder than any Christian I knew.

Think of the most loving, gentle, patient, gracious people you know. The Lord is kinder than them—way kinder. From that moment on, things started to change for me and Josh. I began to break free from shame. Hearing God's words of love

---

* Note: If you or your spouse is experiencing feelings of hopelessness or suicidal ideation, it is important that you know help is available. Call the nationwide suicide crisis line at 988, go to your nearest emergency room, or reach out to a licensed mental health professional.

over me didn't take away the wrong I had done or make me feel any less sorry, but I felt less sorrowful about my soul, life, and outlook. And I experienced hope.

SHAKE OFF SHAME

Do you need God's words over your life? Are you craving His love, grace, compassion, and clarity? This path of having a new marriage is not meant to be done alone. If you are not seeking the God who created you, who knows you and your circumstances better than you know yourself, and who fills you up with love, you will be pouring out from empty vessels.

One of my favorite stories in the Bible that is a great example of how Jesus is kinder than any Christian you know is found in chapter 8 of John's Gospel. Jesus was in the middle of teaching, and the religious leaders came through the crowd saying something like, "Yes, yes, Jesus. Okay, we get it. Have compassion, but what about this . . ." and they threw onto the ground in front of Jesus a woman who had been caught in adultery.

Picture them all surrounding her. Accusing her. Something she had done in private was now very public. She knew she had sinned, and she may have felt convicted even as she was in the act, but the leaders had not brought her to Jesus to give her a chance to repent and be restored. No, they brought her to be accused and condemned.

Maybe you have felt not only the weight of your sin but also the shame that the Enemy wants to heap on your shoulders and make you carry forever. And unfortunately, sometimes he gets help from our fellow Christians, who look down on us with their weaponized biblical truths, moral accusations, personal opinions, and hurtful attacks.

In this woman who was dragged before Jesus, we see ourselves and our sin. And we are aware of our accusers as well. But I pray we also are surprised by Jesus' love for us.

> Then he stooped down again and wrote in the dust. When the accusers heard this, they slipped away one by one, beginning with the oldest, until only Jesus was left in the middle of the crowd with the woman. Then Jesus stood up again and said to the woman, "Where are your accusers? Didn't even one of them condemn you?" "No, Lord," she said. And Jesus said, "Neither do I. Go and sin no more." (John 8:8–11 NLT)

Jesus knows all and holds all of our stories, and His compassion and kindness are unfailing. Hearing and receiving the words He speaks to you at your lowest point should shape and direct your life as you represent Him in your marriage and family as well as your greater community. Remember: the moment you felt farthest from Him, He was closest to you. I will never forget that moment for me.

It's impossible to rebuild from a shame seat. The Enemy is too powerful and holds too much authority when you operate from a place of self-hate, condemnation, and hopelessness. My darkest moment became so pivotal for me and Josh, and we've seen the same in so many other couples since. Once I believed and lived from Jesus' words over me, I began to have the strength to shake off shame. I knew the people whom I admired and trusted were disappointed in me, but because I knew they loved me and were cheering me on, their disappointment didn't keep me isolated or compel me to break off relationships.

It was unbelievable how important it was to know that God loved me. It gave me the confidence to move forward. Now, the next several years were not cupcakes and lollipops—there was still much work required to rebuild and learn to have a new marriage—but this was the first building block.

God is more than enough, and you can ask Him for His promises and faithfulness. Do you know that the God who fashioned and created you is the same one who sustains you when you fall or are brought low? That same love that knit you together, knows every hair on your head, and sets good works in motion for you to walk in never changes. There may be huge walls between us in our marriage—betrayal, wounds, unmet expectations, unforgiveness, and resentment—but God is with us in our hurting and healing.

Proverbs 4:26–27 encourages us to seek wisdom: "Give careful thought to the paths for your feet and be steadfast in all your ways. Do not turn to the right or the left; keep your foot from evil." Focus on God's goodness and His plan for your marriage.

You know, the thing about the marriage covenant is that God designed it. When He made you and knew it was not good for you to be alone, He knew of your future marriage and had your spouse in mind. He knew your strengths and weaknesses; He knew of the sharpening that would have to occur for you to have the lasting love that He desired for you. All marriages go through trials, have shortcomings, have moments where the couple grates on each other's nerves, and we have to choose to walk in this covenant of love time and time again.

From our experience, more marriages than you may think go through deep pains of betrayal, addiction, disappointment, and broken trust. In these situations, the God of mercy, redemption, and grace is up for the task. It's His very nature, and He can't stop loving you. But it's up to you to let Him in. To realize He is not like most Christians we know. He is not waiting to condemn, He is not too disappointed to connect, and He does not need to protect Himself or His pride from you or your shortcomings. He is kinder than any Christian you have ever known, and He is waiting to speak words of life and love over you. And if you are hearing these words for the first time or have been impacted by them at any point in your life, don't forget them. It's the way you will love others through their flaws and points of shame. They need God's love too. And He is kinder than you or I can ever be.

Ten

CELEBRATE THE
MARKERS

You are not alone in your pain and your struggles. We hope that has been made evident to you by now. We all go through seasons where we are unsure how to make it through. But once you have committed to staying and doing the work, be aware that you can suddenly feel like you are moving nowhere fast. In any season of waiting, it's essential to work the plan and stay faithful to those right actions we talked about in chapter 7. However, our lives were meant to be enjoyed and celebrated, and the marriage covenant is intended to encourage couples to share in the highs and lows.

That's why it's essential to mark your progress, no matter how small, and celebrate.

It's always easier to see and celebrate the moments in hindsight; however, we want you to experience the joy that comes from recognizing the little victories in the moment and give yourself the gift of celebrating how God is working in your marriage.

In our story, one of my (Katie's) coping mechanisms with the grief and shame I was experiencing after uncovering my sin publicly was to sleep. I would go to bed early and nap during the day as often as possible to get out of my head and, honestly, out of my present reality. One of the places I exercised this coping mechanism most often was in the car with Josh. I have the spiritual gift of sleeping in any moving vehicle, whether it be a plane, train, or automobile. So the vehicle would start moving, and Josh would be hopeful, I am sure, for some good conversation. But I would drift off to another land, cutting some z's.

I look back now, thinking how hard it must have been for Josh to know I was still escaping, trying to be anywhere but where I was. This tendency to sleep became very important in our story, though, because it was the first time I remember seeing a little progress that I knew was worth celebrating in my soul. It was a Saturday afternoon, and we had loaded up all the kids to drive downtown to Charleston. We were going to walk around the farmers market, run some errands, and then make the drive back to North Charleston, where we lived, about forty minutes away. The day went according to plan, and our three kids at the time loved walking around and looking at the sights and sounds of downtown. I remember it was cool outside and can still picture Annajaye's little hoodie she was wearing in the back seat.

When Josh stopped to run into a store on the way home, Annajaye and Abigail made a video in the back seat while Abel (only six months or so) slept in the car seat. We still have the video, and it helps me remember the moments of this special day. After all the errands, we drove back home, and I clearly remember not sleeping but singing and laughing with the girls and Josh all the way home. That was progress! But, because this book is all about vulnerability and the natural and raw of processes of what rebuilding a marriage looks like, I also have to tell you that at that moment things were still not all well in my heart and soul. As the girls made the video in the back seat, I remember wanting to send it to the other man. I didn't, but I write this so you know how dangerous it is when you give a piece of your heart and soul away. It takes a long time to fully surrender that heart to God, repent, and be back in your covenant.

The truth is, even though that was going on in my heart and I would eventually confess it to Josh, this day was still a marker in our journey and one that needed to be celebrated. We got home that night, and before we fell asleep, Josh told me, "You stayed awake!" Even though I was still operating from the unhealthy place of thinking about the other man, I took the thought captive quickly, didn't send the video, and stayed engaged in our present reality. The biggest thing to celebrate was, I loved it!

RECOGNIZING THE MARKERS

When overcoming hidden sin, you can liken it to withdrawing from something you know is harmful to you. Sometimes we have to break many little addictions—online shopping, binge-watching Netflix, and even eating Oreos, to name a few—to make sure we live and operate in a place of freedom. In all such instances when we seek freedom and teach ourselves to abstain for a time, we find that we can't always control how often these things come to mind. However, we can shorten the time we think about them, confess any sin, and move on. The same is true in the covenant of marriage! You know you are making progress when you spend less time thinking about sinning, when you confess and repent early and often, and most importantly when you stay present to your reality and vow. The process of celebrating the markers is all about taking a moment on the journey to recognize and rejoice over any progress.

We are all at different points on our journey to a thriving marriage. The next (and last) section of the book is all about vision, where we will invite you to dream and even write down what a flourishing marriage means to you. But for now, let's continue to focus on celebrating the markers that show you are making progress.

We want marriages that are in the flow state. You may not use that term, but you have most likely experienced it. When people are "in the flow," they may not notice time passing, think about why they are doing a task, or judge their efforts.

Instead, they remain entirely focused. The flow state in marriage is those seasons when you are less focused on the work and more focused on the joy that comes from trying to out-serve each other. When Josh and I are in flow, there is an ease with which we do life together. We wake up looking for ways to serve, connect, or surprise each other. It's not all romance and flowers, but it's making the bed and brewing the coffee without thinking about who did it last.

Many of you have certainly moved in and out of the flow state before. The truth about a marriage covenant, similar to our relationships with God and others, is that sometimes there is an ease of operation, and other times it can feel like monotony or, worse, drudgery. I want hope to rise in you that it does not have to stay this way. You will get through seasons that feel never-ending and monotonous or hard and challenging and move into seasons where there is more flow and joy.

In celebrating the markers, call things good when they are good, and don't move on too quickly. When you find yourself operating in the flow and working well with each other, that's also a great time to create new goals as a couple. Maybe during these nonconflict times, you take up a new hobby together, focus on your sexual intimacy, or start a new mission-focused service project. You are in a flow for a reason, and it's a great time to celebrate that and work toward your vision and long-term goals.

For those who can't imagine a flow state because your current season feels too challenging and full of hardship, celebrating the markers is even more critical. You may need a magnifying glass to see any hope, joy, and contentment in the now, but celebrating even the tiniest of markers is your path. Perhaps journaling would be handy in this process, because how will you know what to celebrate and how far you have come if you don't write it down? No matter where you are on the journey, give yourself time to think about your pain points and one thing you would like to change. Like, for me, staying awake in the car!

CREATING NEW MARKERS

Coming out of our season of counseling, we knew that we needed to have consistent date nights. Those were markers that we could create, celebrating them in the moment. We didn't have the finances, so we started praying and asking if someone was willing to invest in our marriage and help us with babysitting. You would be surprised how many older couples would love to help and support you in a tough season with childcare as they remember people who were there for them when they needed it. My mom and stepdad agreed to continue keeping the kids, and once our counseling ended, our first marker was to have weekly date nights. The second goal was not to fight through them. My sister and brother-in-law have a rule of no bad date nights; if they fight through one, they will schedule another one to make up for it. Once we started having consistent date nights, we celebrated that and never stopped.

A couple of years ago, we wanted to go to a new place in our health and excitement for date nights, so we decided not to let ourselves have anything alcoholic to drink until date night. You can imagine how much we longed for date night and celebrated the mess out of it. One, we were proud of our efforts toward freedom and health, and two, we couldn't wait to spend time with each other and have fun; it was a marker. Neither of us drinks alcohol at this moment and we are trying to eat healthily, so we still try to make date nights fun with new activities and creative ideas to play together. Last night we went to Whole Foods and then to look at books in Barnes & Noble. We had a blast together, and Josh is my favorite person! This is worth celebrating.

What marker are you being prompted to think about while reading this? What do you want to go after next, and what can you celebrate on the journey there? I have run exactly two half-marathons in my life, so all real runners, please look past my obvious lack of experience, but the same principles apply. When you set out to run for any length of time, it is important to know the distance you are trying to go and then celebrate not just when you complete it but also mark the path along the way. If you are setting out to run 13.1 miles—or I can imagine even more so with 26.2 miles—you need a plan for the markers and how you will take the journey.

When preparing for my most recent half-marathon, I had this plan down. I started the first three miles with no music and no talking to my partner, just taking it slow and easy and letting my body settle into the long journey. Once I got to mile 3, the plan was to have a casual conversation with my running partner. We still took things slowly, but we were letting ourselves mentally go somewhere else for the next three. Now we were all about the markers, attacking mile 6 with a little more passion and speed. We called it our fun mile, taking us up and over the halfway hill.

Coming into mile 7, we told ourselves the entire time to enjoy and celebrate being over halfway done, letting our bodies feel the endorphins but also staying slow and pulling back. At mile 7, we started the playlist we created and enjoyed the soundtrack that would take us through the end of the race. I remember celebrating so much when that music came on, and I was ready to go inward and enjoy the run on my own by that point. It was invigorating and just what I needed to get me to mile 9, where our kids would be waiting to cheer us on.

The motivation from family carried us until mile 10, which is the first time I remember feeling the difficulty of running this long race. I kept looking and looking for the mile 11 but never saw it. I needed the marker desperately! My friend and I began slowing down and feeling fatigued, but when we rounded a corner, you can imagine our delight when we read *mile 12*! We had missed an entire marker, but we were in our final mile! We called this final mile the freedom mile, because we knew it wouldn't be long till we were celebrating at the finish line!

Just as not every race is the same, not every marriage is the same. Hills, turns, and heat vary, and you need to plan out your course according to your specific circumstances and goals. These principles that are required in any goal or area where you are stretching yourself apply in marriage all the more! Why do we forget in the marathon of our covenant that we need a plan for every season, and the plan needs to include markers where we can stop and celebrate, regroup, or refocus?

Whether you are in a slightly challenging or devastatingly difficult season in your covenant, you can get through it, and you can endure. I know you can because I have lived through the worst hell and brokenness marriages can endure and watched God do miracles in our covenant. I have also been in seasons that moved in and out of flow state, where we found ways to celebrate and markers to journal about, which were a light to lead us back home. There are seasons of grief and hardship when you need time and patient endurance to begin to feel like yourselves again; recognize and celebrate time markers of three and six months out, one year out, three years out, five years out, and keep celebrating your endurance of supporting each other through those seasons.

MARK YOUR EBENEZER

You are not rare because your covenant had or is having trials, hardships, or seasons where nothing feels enjoyable in your marriage. You are rare because as a couple you aren't just enduring these times but you are celebrating your progress through them. Together you can have hope and give thanks. The way to do that is by celebrating the markers.

God is the author and perfector of this principle of celebrating markers. In the Bible are stories of the people of Israel setting up Ebenezers, or stone markers, as reminders that God has been with them and helped them through. Here is one story in 1 Samuel where Ebenezer is used:

Then all the people of Israel turned back to the LORD. So Samuel said to all the Israelites, "If you are returning to the LORD with all your hearts, then rid yourselves of the foreign gods and the Ashtoreths and commit yourselves to the LORD and serve him only, and he will deliver you out of the hand of the Philistines." So the Israelites put away their Baals and Ashtoreths, and served the LORD only. . . . While Samuel was sacrificing the burnt offering, the Philistines drew near to engage Israel in battle. But that day the LORD thundered with loud thunder against the Philistines and threw them into such a panic that they were routed before the Israelites. . . .

Then Samuel took a stone and set it up between Mizpah and Shen. He named it Ebenezer, saying, "Thus far the LORD has helped us." So the Philistines were subdued and they stopped invading Israel's territory. Throughout Samuel's lifetime, the hand of the LORD was against the Philistines. The towns from Ekron to Gath that the Philistines had captured from Israel were restored to Israel, and Israel delivered the neighboring territory from the hands of the Philistines. And there was peace between Israel and the Amorites. Samuel continued as

Israel's leader all the days of his life. From year to year he went on a circuit from Bethel to Gilgal to Mizpah, judging Israel in all those places. But he always went back to Ramah, where his home was, and there he also held court for Israel. And he built an altar there to the LORD. (7:2–4, 10, 12–17)

I love this story for many reasons. Mainly, the people finally woke up to the fact that they could not win battles on their own. They needed God all along, but in this moment they were very aware of that fact. They did not have what it took to beat the foreign armies or conquer their land. After they had repented of their sins and committed themselves to serving only God, that's when the enemy attacked them.

Have you ever been there? Or are you there now? You wanted to seek God and be used by Him in your covenant and never thought you would find yourself unable to withstand the Enemy and his schemes to destroy your marriage. Josh and I certainly have. In this moment of humility before the Lord, you admit you need Him to rescue, redeem, and restore your covenant, and He gets the most glory.

Samuel knew this and continued to seek God on the Israelites' behalf. Once they won the battle through thunder and confusion, a tactic delivered only by God, Samuel wanted to make sure they celebrated with a marker.

In your marriage, you will have markers along your journey that only God can explain. Perhaps God is asking you to set up an Ebenezer, or a marker, that commemorates His work in your lives during these times. My mom has an Ebenezer wall. Surrounding a pond is a wall built by medium-sized stones on which she has written Ebenezer moments that God has brought our family through. This past year on her thirtieth wedding anniversary, she and my stepdad had a vow renewal service where us three kids, her sons-in-law, and all eleven grandkids read out the moments on the stones that only God could get the credit for. On a brick by the pond is written, "God saving and restoring Josh and Katie's marriage. 2008." A marker that we will never stop thanking Him for.

God is asking us to celebrate the markers in the small wins through each and every season. Write down what you are hoping for and what you are seeking to celebrate on this long journey to a thriving marriage. When you get through a tough season and look back on major events He has taken you through that only He can get the credit for, mark your Ebenezer. It doesn't have to be a wall made of stone, but make it prominent so it can be made known. "Thus far the Lord has helped us!" If He is for you, who can be against you? It's time to celebrate!

Part Four

START WITH ME

TAKE QUITTING
OFF THE TABLE

ALLOW OTHERS TO BE
A PART OF THE STORY

YIELD TO VISION

To make a marriage last a lifetime, you need vision. You need a destination, an image in your mind, a goal to cling to. It's common to talk about vision when it comes to leading a ministry or building a business, but it's equally important in our personal lives. What do you want out of this marriage? What do you want things to look like in fifty years? What is the whole point of it? Marriages are unique, like people, and yielding to a vision for your unique marriage is the crucial last part of the S.T.A.Y. acronym. This requires faith, a sense of imagination, and even a little fun.

JUST AROUND
THE CORNER

To reason about something is to take a look at it from multiple angles and then come to a conclusion based on an informed and logical analysis. Have you ever made a decision that you later looked back on and asked yourself, *Why did I think that was a good decision?* Often in these situations, which seem to lack any sense of reasoning, you probably weren't experiencing any positive, refreshing, or life-giving emotions, and you were searching for something that would feel good. You may not have realized it at the time, but truth be told, you were on a treasure hunt, hoping that a certain decision or action would help you feel better.

Consider this equation:

I discover my wife has had an affair.
+ I lose my job.
+ We move our family to a new city.
+ We have a home for sale in Columbia.
+ We are renting a house in Charleston.
+ I am unemployed.
= The ideal time to buy my dream car on eBay.

Looking back, I remember being genuinely excited about the idea and thinking, *This is going to be great!* Katie and I were struggling to connect. She was working as a guidance counselor and was gone each day from seven thirty to three thirty. I was still staying home with the kids, picking up odd jobs as I could find them, and looking for work. She'd come home, tired from her day and worn out by the idea of trying to enjoy life at home with me. My reasoning for making the purchase was that we needed a vehicle. That said, it's never a good idea to buy your dream car when you are unemployed. It's just not the best time to take on new debt. Oh, and did I mention we had to pick it up in Scottsdale, Arizona?

As Katie mentioned earlier, she has the spiritual gift of sleeping while I drive (no, you won't find this one listed in Scripture, though it's so powerful it must be from God). There have been many trips where she's knocked out before we even pull out of the neighborhood. Driving back from Scottsdale after picking up the car would have us stuck together for four days; we'd see some beautiful places and have plenty of time to talk in a sweet new ride. Our flow would look something like this: she could sleep first; then we could talk, have some adventures, sleep, talk, have some experiences; again, this was going to be great! I purchased one-way tickets to Arizona and we were off.

Upon landing, we decided to drive north to the Grand Canyon to see the sunset before turning east and heading home. Neither of us had ever been to the Grand Canyon, nor had I researched the various rims or views to prioritize if you are passing through. We picked up the car and drove north on State Route 64 toward the South Rim. As sunset drew closer, I started making turns toward what looked like the giant hole on the map, also known as the Grand Canyon. At one point, I could sense we were running out of time. Katie was already exercising her spiritual gift; I was driving up a long, straight road surrounded by tall trees on both sides. I didn't see any signs of beauty or imagery I'd remotely call *grand*, and I was starting to wonder if this had been a waste of time.

At one point, I started seeing Caution signs due to a hard turn in the road, making it clear to slow down. As we approached the curve, the landscape opened up, and in a moment we went from an underwhelming ride through the woods to one of the most glorious views I'd ever seen, driving along the rim of the canyon just in time for sunset. As we turned, God spoke to me, saying, *That's how quickly your story can change. New life is just around the corner.* It was so powerful. The contrast in scenery and the reality of my emotions wrecked me. I started crying to the degree that it startled Katie. She woke up screaming,

"What's wrong? What happened?" I pulled over to share what God had said, pull myself together, and give us a minute to take in the view. It was a moment that changed everything.

Side note: God accounted for my lack of reasoning. We finally made it home, enjoyed the ride, and sold the car a year later on eBay for the same price we'd purchased it . . . to a couple living in Scottsdale, Arizona! They bought a one-way ticket to Charleston, picked it up, and drove it back across the country.

THE PROMISE

Think of a time when you were in a season that made you question whether things would ever change. Maybe you're in one now. *Will he ever look at me the way he used to? Will she ever respect me? Will we ever have another conversation that doesn't end up in a fight or one of us checking out? Will I ever look forward to date night instead of feeling apprehensive about it? Can this situation ever get better? Will I ever stop feeling this way?*

I tend to be an optimist. I know God is loving, kind, and powerful. He has good in store for us and can do anything, anytime. I genuinely believe that, though I remember my pain in that season being so great that it was starting to eat away at my belief that God would heal our marriage. I knew He could, but it hadn't happened yet, and I was growing weary. I wasn't going anywhere; I wasn't giving up; I was just tired and losing hope, until I heard from God at the edge of the Grand Canyon. Hearing from God renewed my hope. From that day forward, I woke up each morning questioning, *Is today the day?* When Katie got home from work, *Is this the moment?* I was confident new life was just around the corner, that it could happen in a moment.

Our landscape can change entirely—what looks dull and dead can become beautiful and vibrant. In Luke 2:10 an angel appeared to some shepherds out in a field to announce the birth of Jesus. They were startled by its appearance, but the angel said, "Do not be afraid. I bring you good news that will cause great joy for all the people." I've heard my pastor, Greg Surratt, say, "Good news becomes a great joy when it becomes personal." The thought that our story could change in a moment, that new life was just around the corner, was merely encouraging words until they became personal.

The reality of this promise is available to all of us. Especially to you as a couple going through difficult times. Throughout Scripture, there are stories of men and women who were in seemingly desperate situations and had been for some time, only for God to show up in a moment, flip the script, and do what seemed impossible in their lives.

- Daniel was delivered from the lion's den (Daniel 6).
- Shadrach, Meshach, and Abednego emerged untouched from the fiery furnace (Daniel 3).
- Joseph was betrayed, sold into slavery, framed, thrown into prison, and emerged as the second-in-command in all of Egypt (Genesis 37, 39, 41).
- Esther was positioned by God to boldly go before the king to help bring about deliverance for the Jews.

Over and over, we see men and women who had faced impossible situations overcome them due to one driving attribute: hope. They had hope in the unfailing, all-powerful, ever-present God they served. The lives and circumstances of people in the Bible can seem so distant and different from ours that it can be hard to relate to them. However, the emotional and mental anguish through which they persevered is captured in the Word of God as a source of vision and inspiration for us. Because they had hope, you and I can as well.

Second Corinthians 1:3–4 says, "Praise be to the God and Father of our Lord Jesus Christ, the Father of compassion and the God of all comfort, who comforts us in all our troubles, so that we can comfort those in any trouble with the comfort we ourselves receive from God." God met me amid my troubles, in the moments when my faith was fading, to restore my hope.

I thought flying across the country to pick up a car was about making a new memory, having a conversation, and picking up a means of transportation. In reality, though, it was a modern-day parable meant to restore my hope that I might be able to pass on the following few lessons to help renew yours.

DON'T SETTLE FOR STUFF

Katie has been known to tell me that I get "fixated" on something. It drives me crazy; I wouldn't say I like that word. If it's a need around the house, a project to get done, or a possession to be obtained, I can become narrowly focused on it. In my idle moments, I'm researching Facebook Marketplace, reading reviews, hunting down the best deal, or working on getting it done—whatever *it* may be. There is something about acquiring the item or checking off the task that feels good. The pursuit of stuff is all about gaining something outside of me in hopes that it will bring about satisfaction on the inside of me.

In seasons of pain, anytime we avoid what is happening on the inside to attain or accomplish something outside ourselves, it only prolongs our healing process. Proverbs 13:12 says, "Hope deferred makes the heart sick, but a desire fulfilled is a tree of life" (ESV). There is only one in whom we can put our hope, and His name is Jesus.

When we hitch our hope to the things of this world, it will leave our hearts sick. Colossians 3:2 says, "Set your minds on things above, not on earthly things." Throughout Scripture, God and the things of God are commonly referenced as "above," which is powerful because of the sense of direction it demands. If I told you the item you were looking for was above you, you'd naturally look up. No longer would you waste time looking at whoever or whatever is beside, in front of, or behind you.

Jesus spoke to this in Matthew 6:33; His counsel was to "seek first the kingdom of God and his righteousness" (ESV). The language used in Colossians 3:2 is comparable; most Bible translations are a slight variation on "Set your mind on things above," but the original language more accurately reads, "keep seeking."[1]

Amid the pain, anything you can attain on your own is probably not worth keeping. Stay focused. What are you seeking first and most? If you seek God first and often, He will bring about the healing you need.

DON'T GET LOST IN THE TREES

Have you ever heard the saying, "They can't see the forest for the trees"? It refers to someone so focused on the details that they can't see the big picture. What's difficult about this saying is how the person in the middle of the forest, or the "middle of the mess," applies it. I'm thinking, *By all means, someone, please show me the forest; I'd love to see the bigger picture. But for now, I'm surrounded by trees.* Our position determines our perspective, and when we are physically close to the challenges we face, our challenges and difficulties are all we see.

When you're hiking in the forest, it's easy to grow weary. You feel the intensity of ascending and descending the path, the sweat on your brow, and the swelling of your feet. You are very aware of your experience and the impact it's having on you. In the forest, you don't get anywhere fast. More times than not, you're wearing a pack, carrying baggage of some kind, and you are slowly moving forward. One. Step. At. A. Time. Heaven forbid you go the wrong direction or take the wrong path, only to find yourself needing to backtrack, wasting more time and energy, and then starting over . . . one step at a time. If that wasn't enough, pain can make you feel as if you're on the journey all alone. You tend to run into friends at the grocery store, not in the forest.

When you are walking through a season of pain, the forest or the great outdoors can feel a lot more like a wilderness experience than a long walk in the woods. Two phrases that have a lot in common are "great outdoors" and "wilderness camp." If you google them together, you'll get more than seventy-six million results.

That said, the two often describe very different experiences—just ask the children of Israel between Egypt and the promised land. "How did you feel about eating manna for forty years while in the wilderness?" Sure, it was bread from heaven that God provided daily for nourishment, but you would not likely hear testimonies rolling in of how much they enjoyed "the great outdoors." The wilderness was what they felt, what they saw, and what they experienced. The reality of the trees, the forest God was trying to show them, had nothing to do with the landscape but the Source of their provision. He had to teach them that their nourishment came from their Maker and that they could trust and obey Him day by day, step-by-step.

It's easy to comment on another person's marriage journey because we can often see what they can't see, observing their forest but empathizing with what it feels like to be lost in the trees. It's also easy to look back on our own forest and see things clearly after we've made it through the trees. The question for us, then, is how do we keep from getting lost in the foliage? How do we keep from focusing on the details? When you've been hurt, when trust has been broken, when every short response, off look, harsh tone, or failure to follow through becomes an unavoidable tree, a painful detail on which to fixate, it can be challenging. Much like the children of Israel, we learn to remember God's fulfilled promises and then to trust and obey His plan.

For example, when my thoughts are negative and critical, I try to apply this scripture: "Finally, brothers and sisters, whatever is true, whatever is noble, whatever is right, whatever is pure, whatever is lovely, whatever is admirable—if anything is excellent or praiseworthy—think about such things" (Phil. 4:8). When I'm tempted to raise my voice in anger, I recall that "a soft answer turns away wrath, but a harsh word stirs up anger" (Prov. 15:1 ESV). Do I want to resolve this argument or stir the pot? When I'm tempted to fight Katie for what I think I deserve, I'm reminded, "Husbands, love your wives, just as Christ loved the church and gave himself up for her" (Eph. 5:25).

When we are lost in the trees, often the way out is to start asking questions instead of making accusations. *God, where are we going? What are You trying to teach me? What am I not seeing? What did I miss? What do I need to own? What do I need to repent of? Apologize for?* This helps us to trust and obey God. He is allowing you to see the trees for a reason. He wants to meet you in your place of pain and then lead you through the woods. As He reveals His love to you, you will walk out of the forest more confident of His love, power, and presence in your life. But it will happen one step at a time, as you trust and obey.

During this deep-in-the-woods marriage season, Katie and I lacked intimacy and connection. We felt more like roommates than lovers or best friends. Not because I didn't want it or we weren't trying; she just wasn't feeling it. There was a fair amount of smiling and laughter in the home, but it was usually associated with the kids. We were tired of looking at the same ole trees and in desperate need of a change.

How do you feel about change? New things? New places? Does it excite you? Does it stress you out? If driving the same roads, going to the same places, and hanging with the same people played a part in getting us where we are, how can we expect change if we don't allow God to take us to new places?

God wanted to do a new work in Abram's life, telling him, "I will make you into a great nation, and I will bless you; I will make your name great, and you will be a blessing" (Gen. 12:2). If I'm Abram, I'm thinking, *Wow. That's amazing, God. Let's do this!* But first Abram had to move forward—and move to a foreign land—in obedience and in faith.

Is there a church, a neighborhood, a city, a state, a counselor, or a group of friends that God is calling you to? That's where Katie and I were led. When you move forward in faith, looking beyond the tree in front of your nose, God will guide you to many new things and ultimately bring about a new work in your marriage.

PULL OVER TO TAKE IN THE VIEW

When was the last time you saw something so beautiful that you had to give your full attention to it? I've got dozens of pictures in my phone of beautiful sunsets that I captured while driving up the interstate or over a bridge around town. Charleston County is essentially a series of islands connected by bridges. Anytime you are driving over a bridge at sunset, it's not unusual for the sun, sky, and water to come together and create a painting that has you pulling out your phone at forty-five miles per hour to catch a pic.

As I scroll through pictures of the beautiful sunsets I've captured over the years, while many of them may jog a memory of where I was or when I saw it, few are marking moments. There are two sunsets, however, that I'll never forget. One happened on the Grand Canyon trip and another while Katie and I were on vacation in Maui. In both cases, we pulled over, got out of the car, and took some time to take in the view. In Maui, we may or may not have turned up the radio and had a sunset dance party on the side of the road.

The nature of our lives and marriages is a process of transformation. We are going from death to life and daily being formed more and more into the image of Christ. Throughout the New Testament, the Greek word used for "transform" is *metamorphoo*,[2] which means to change into another form. It is used four times in Scripture, two of which are about Jesus (Matt. 17:2 and Mark 9:2) and two in reference to you and me:

> Do not conform to the pattern of this world, but be *transformed* by the renewing of your mind. Then you will be able to test and approve what God's will is—his good, pleasing and perfect will. (Rom. 12:2, emphasis added)

And we all, who with unveiled faces contemplate the Lord's glory, are being *transformed* into his image with ever-increasing glory, which comes from the Lord, who is the Spirit. (2 Cor. 3:18, emphasis added)

The Spirit of God in us is constantly at work, bringing beauty to our lives. The word picture of *glory* in 2 Corinthians is translated as "splendor" or "brightness," about the moon, sun, or stars.[3] In other words, when we walk closely with God, we should experience moments where we catch a glimpse of ourselves or those we love, and instead of grabbing a pic in passing, we should pull over and make a moment of it: Journal about the fruit God has brought about and the change He's authored in our lives to help us remember who we were and who we are. Grab a coffee or sit down across from those in whom we see a change and tell them what we see God doing in them. Write a card, shoot a text, and create a memory that serves as a milestone in our transformation. Purposefully pulling over to take in the beauty.

The exciting thing about transformation that resembles how God brings about beauty in our lives is that for something beautiful to emerge, there are things about the old appearance that must die. Consider the metamorphosis of a butterfly: "One day, the caterpillar stops eating, hangs upside down from a twig or leaf and spins itself a silky cocoon or molts into a shiny chrysalis. Within its protective casing, the caterpillar radically transforms its body, eventually emerging as a butterfly or moth."[4] The slow-crawling and unattractive caterpillar has to die to be transformed into the flying, fast, and beautiful butterfly.

As we walk with God, He will also bring about the same degree of transformation in our lives. It is the call of a Christ follower. In Luke 9:23 Jesus said, "Whoever wants to be my disciple must deny themselves and take up their cross daily and follow me." To be identified with Christ, there will be areas of our lives where we are called to die daily. It's also a husband's call; Ephesians 5:25 says, "Husbands, love your wives, just as Christ loved the church and gave himself up for her." In our world, death is devastating and feels final. In the kingdom of God, however, death is the gateway to beauty. When you pull over to take in the beauty, it's a powerful reminder that we aren't who we used to be. God's not done; He's still at work.

HAVE HOPE FOR TODAY

When was the last time you walked through something where you used the word *endure* to describe your experience? I'm reminded of the home renovations we've completed, past jobs, and our marriage crisis. Sometimes endurance is scheduled and momentary. Needing to get through a workout or complete a tough job, you know the finish line is within reach, so you push through the pain to get it done. But sometimes endurance is needed over a season, when you aren't sure when or if the pain will end. It's in those moments when our hope is tested. I've heard past performance is the best indicator of future results. When you see little to no improvement over time, the temptation is to believe that things will continue to be the way they have always been. In other words, my future will be a similar version of my current reality.

By nature, I'm an unrepentant optimist. I believe tomorrow will be better, regardless of what today feels like. There aren't many challenges that can't be turned around in due time with hard work, a good attitude, and the grace of God. That said, I remember moments four to five months into this season of our marriage where I felt what psychotherapist Lesley Alderman calls "hope fatigue." Longing for an end to the 2020 pandemic, unity in our country, and resolution to war globally, she coined the term to describe weary people struggling with a "deficit of optimism."[5]

There are days when positivity and optimism can help you believe the best, see the silver lining, and continue moving forward. But amid a crisis when you need a miracle, even natural optimism can become obsolete. The only way to maintain unfailing and authentic hope is by examining the source of your hope. If your hope stems from a willingness to work hard and a dogged belief that things will get better, in time you will likely grow weary, and your ability to endure will fade. But if your hope for today is found in Jesus—if you are seeking, praying, and believing that He can do the heavy lifting, He can change hearts, He can bring unity, that He is the miracle worker in your marriage—then you won't take that mantle on yourself.

In 1 Thessalonians 1:3, Paul said, "We remember before our God and Father your work produced by faith, your labor prompted by love, and your endurance inspired by hope in our Lord Jesus Christ." *Work*, *labor*, and *endurance* are words we are very familiar with in American culture. Paul's language gives us the formula to help us hope for today; they serve as a powerful guide to prayer.

- *"Your work produced by faith."* Don't try fixing your marriage on your own. God is with you, God is for you, God will help you. So, the best place to start is in prayer. Ask God to show you how to work on the relationship this week. May faith produce every card you write, flower you purchase, note you leave, and text you send to your spouse. Believe that God is moving, working, and leading you to better serve and care for each other. Your faithfulness will bear fruit.

- *"Your labor prompted by love."* God loved the world so much that He gave His only Son to save us (John 3:16). God's love prompted Jesus' presence on earth, which was all about serving rather than being served (Matt. 20:28). In humility, Jesus loved those who rejected Him. He washed the feet of His disciples and positioned Himself as a servant. Today, for every dish you wash, bed you make, car you clean, errand you run, or bill you pay, ask God to help you to serve in humility, prompted by His example and love.

- *"Your endurance inspired by hope in our Lord Jesus Christ."* Don't get weary of working; just because it feels like labor doesn't mean you are losing. Pray that your hope in our Lord Jesus will inspire you to endure. I often picture Him on the cross, praying for those who crucified Him. He paid the ultimate price for you and me; He finished the job. Ask the Holy Spirit to empower you today so that you will endure the challenges you face because of your hope in Jesus.

Anytime you are driving up the road and approaching a corner, there are likely two realities at play. First, you cannot see what's around the corner. There are trees, buildings, or structures of some kind blocking your view. You lack vision, but you keep moving forward in faith, believing that the curve in the road will take you from where you've been to where you're headed. The second reality is that you'll have to adjust your speed. You can't navigate the corner at the same rate you've been driving. That could be very dangerous. The curve in the road is a transition zone, taking you in a new direction.

I don't know what season you are walking through or how much faith you have that new life is just around the corner, but if you'll keep moving forward in faith and slow down a bit, I'm confident God will take you to a new place, bless you, and do a new thing in your marriage.

Twelve

LET HIM DO A
NEW THING

I remember two points of our story like they were yesterday, so vastly different and surprising looking back. After that terrible night when I thought about ending my life but heard God's kind, loving words drawing me to Him, Josh and I went to church the following day at the Seacoast Dream Center. The service was incredible, and it felt like everything—the worship and message—was made for our exact season of pain. Afterward, I remember going to the front altar with Josh and telling the pastor our entire story. I finally felt free enough to say the words because I had been encouraged by the words of a loving God. With tears running down our faces, when I confessed to an affair almost ruining our marriage, the pastor looked at us with this incredible strength and said, "Me too." *Me too* are powerful words.

He pointed to his wife and children on the front row and said twenty years ago they were in a similar situation, but look at what God has done. That was all he had to say; I didn't need to know the details of his story to feel the hope and inspiration that started to spring up in me, thinking, *I wonder if that could be us.*

Hope is like oxygen in times of crisis, and I believe God orchestrated this moment to give us a deep breath that we so desperately needed. However, two hours later, I experienced a bit of confusion, shock, and discouragement when I spoke with my sister. You see, Jess is my best friend, although it hadn't always been that way growing up; I was a pretty miserable sister, much less a friend. When we both were grown and became believers, though, we instantly made up for the lost time of childhood. During the darkest season of our story, when I was hiding from Josh and friends, she was included in that. Even though at this time she was across the country from me in Seattle, we would FaceTime almost daily. My marriage crisis had been challenging for her because of her deep love for Josh and my persistent hiding things. Early on when news of my affair came out and she was hearing stories from Josh that were different from what I was telling her, it was all too much for her to handle, especially living so far away. Then later when she found out from Josh or my mom about another truth I was hiding, she was hurt, mad, and disgusted all at the same time. So when I called her that afternoon following the church service, my level of enthusiasm and hope was not returned.

I immediately started the conversation with, "Well, Jess, God has changed me and healed me, and I know He will use this story for good. I don't know when, but we will be preaching about this moment. He loves me and has great plans for my life." I'm smiling right now as I write this because I remember it as if it were yesterday, and I also remember Jess's response that I'm sure was accompanied by a massive eye roll that I could feel in Charleston.

I get it, though. There is a lot of pain to walk through, and the healing was still very much in process. When facing a considerable marriage trial or betrayal, two things can happen. The first is *premature confidence* that things will change, and change quickly. The second is too much *delayed hope*, which can allow your hard days to overwhelm you.

For me, delayed hope happened five years after my confession, when God had done tremendous healing in our hearts and story. Josh and I were meeting with another couple walking through a similar pain, and I knew after counseling them for a couple of weeks that five years was too soon to be a healer for others. I started comparing our marriage struggles to theirs, rating how bad my betrayal or sin was in comparison and feeling a bit self-righteous. I knew this was not healthy for my heart, because even a hint of self-righteousness one minute will be full of shame the next. One of the Enemy's most effective tactics with humanity is to keep us on the pendulum swing of judgment—from lamenting, "I'm beyond hope" on one end to flippantly claiming, "Grace covers all" on the other. This keeps us from the ultimate judgment line that falls right at the center: "There is no one righteous, not even one. . . . For all have sinned and fall short of the glory of God" (Rom. 3:10, 23). Under God's love, this leaves us right where He wants us: standing in judgment but believing in forgiveness and redemption because of the cross.

Once we finished counseling that first couple, I knew I needed more time before I was ready to minister out of our pain and healing. I was asked to preach at my first church-sponsored women's event a month later, and I cried through the entire message. I was hoping to break the shame of others and point them to Jesus, but as I shared the pain and the brokenness from our marriage, I realized how fresh the shame and sadness were for me.

STEP-BY-STEP TOWARD YOUR GOAL

There is a time and season for everything (Eccl. 3:1), but if you want a new marriage and have decided to embark on this journey of staying and growing, then you must determine what is the new thing God wants to do and where He wants to begin. I believe with all my heart that marriage and lasting love is a great gift God gives the human heart and soul. The marriage covenant allows for change, security, growth, stability, passion, and promise. No two people are more poised and ready to let God do a new thing in them than two people committed first to God and then to each other.

If you are a business owner or project manager, an athlete or a hiker, or anyone that sets goals, you probably celebrate your accomplishments. If you have ever set a goal to accomplish a new thing, break a bad habit, or change a lifestyle, you know how challenging it can be and how achieving your goal can be nearly impossible if you don't have clear steps for what you will do or stop doing to achieve it. You understand that big goals must be broken down into smaller, more attainable goals that can then be broken down by weekly, daily, and hourly steps.

The same must be true when we let God do a new thing in us and our marriage. We must be clear about what we are asking, how much time we will devote to achieving a chosen goal, and what right actions we will take while we wait for God to do what only He can.

I never dreamed God could restore my passion and emotion for Josh; I thought, at best, I would end up with a chum or pal. So my very first goal was not overly ambitious. I did not expect myself to immediately become attracted to Josh again and have butterflies every time he walked into the room. I could not control this. So instead, I purposely started thinking about which actions or behaviors of his were attractive to me, training myself to recognize and acknowledge the good in him, the things I once loved about him. I then broke this down into daily, weekly, and monthly action steps for one month at a time. I was hoping by the end of month one, I would see growth in this area and could celebrate the progress along the way.

What is one goal you could have for your marriage to feel or look "new" in the next month? Maybe yours is to have more intimacy, not yell so much, be more patient and get less annoyed, increase your desire to spend time together, be a better teammate or partner—the list can go on, but your first step needs to be something that you can control. Don't make a goal that you can't come up with behaviors to support. Then break your goal down into daily, weekly, and monthly actions or behaviors. The following example lists the steps I took to become attracted to Josh again:

Daily:

- Pray for God to restore my attraction to the husband of my youth.
- Think about Josh in a loving way for ten minutes a day.
- Smile at Josh whenever he comes into the room.
- When I see Josh, say something in my mind like, *How am I so blessed?* or *Other women would kill to be his wife*—something to reframe my thoughts.
- Touch Josh whenever he is close.
- Hug Josh five seconds longer than usual.

Weekly:

- Set aside weekly or biweekly time for intimacy.
- Work to be fully present and engaged in conversations.

- Have a weekly date night where I act like a girlfriend—fun and flirty.
- Worship together.

Monthly:

- Have a time on the calendar for one night away that includes fun day dates where we do things we loved in the beginning of our relationship.
- Write Josh a letter telling him how grateful I am for him.

You get the idea.

To let God do a new thing, write down your goal—the new thing you are hoping for. Then break down the action steps that you are responsible for and pray with faith that as you take these right actions, God will do what only He can do!

Here is the most important part: celebrate the markers, just like we learned to do in chapter 10. When you look back and realize you are stronger, healthier, and have more clarity than the season or month before, you will need to celebrate this.

LET HOPE ARISE AND GUIDE

When you have a moment like I did at the very beginning of our crisis, when you feel hope rise, let it! Let God do a new thing, but let Him direct you where to begin. And one day, if you have a moment like I did five years later, where you realize you are stuck in an old thought, behavior, or pattern of thinking, ask Him to do another new thing by taking you to a greater place of strength.

Looking back, I can see why this was important for our progress. It was all about me and Josh yielding to vision. Letting God decide when to do the new thing in your marriage and celebrating along the way is one of the essential parts of becoming a couple who is running toward your vision.

Around seven years following our marriage crisis moment, God gave me the vision to start a fashion line out of Togo, West Africa. The story of how this all began could probably be its own book. Still, the *Reader's Digest* version is, when I had given up on all my dreams of being a missionary and surrendered them instead to being a pastor's wife and mom of five, that's when God allowed me to go to Togo on my first trip overseas in ten years. While there, I heard a lot about impoverished people's lives being changed by having access to a global market for their businesses. Most of the time, I let all that business talk go over my head and instead spent my time planning a counseling trip I led the following year. However, I've always loved fashion, and when I saw the beautiful clothes worn in Togo, I began drawing dresses I wanted to have made.

When I got home, I began dreaming about a company that would empower women and help break generational poverty. A couple of weeks later, I pitched the idea to Pastor Francis Avoyi from Togo, who just happened to be in the US at a teaching conference about a six-hour drive from me.

We raised $15,000 from people in my church and took four hundred preorders to employ our first three seamstresses part-time in Pastor Avoyi's home that he shares with his wife, Benedict. I never could have dreamed what God would do with my small vision, which became the company Francis + Benedict. Seven years later, we have fifteen full-time employees, a thirty-thousand-square-foot shop that we own, and 250 advocates in the United States who sell these skirts online.

The overall vision has always been the same: empowering women to get out of poverty in Togo, West Africa, but it has shifted about a thousand times. If the vision comes to pass, it will outlast me and my children, and I can't imagine how many shapes the vision will take along the way.

If you want to yield to your vision for a new marriage, you will have to let it change and take new forms. God can do more than any of us ask or imagine, so it is so important to stand in faith and celebrate the markers along the way. It's His plan, His healing, His hope . . . so no one is celebrated more than Him.

God designed you, and you have entered this covenant, willing to be made new. Most of us didn't know that this process includes death, at least not so many deaths along the way. However, because of our faithful God, who is more committed to our vision than we are, we can surrender and trust that every time we die to self, a new hope arises. And any change that needs to happen will help us become who He meant for us to be, both individually and as a couple. Each of you holds a piece of your destiny. Let Him do a new thing!

Thirteen

YOUR BEST DAYS
ARE AHEAD

*I*n April 2013, Katie and I purchased our first home in Charleston. It was a foreclosure that had been vacant for nearly two years. There had been squatters living in the house, and just about every wall on the second floor had been used as a canvas for children to draw or paint anything they could imagine. Pets had been locked up in the house for some time and were allowed to use the restroom wherever they needed. After the people moved out, windows had been broken, allowing teenagers to sneak in and throw house parties.

Broken windows also allowed in rain whenever it stormed, causing windows, framing, and flooring to rot. If you wonder whether it was that bad, check the hashtag #3184Linksland on Instagram when you finish reading this chapter.

I'll never forget the first time our real estate agent took us to see the house. We needed something in Mount Pleasant, South Carolina, with five bedrooms that was no more than $250,000. In other words, we were looking for a unicorn. The bank had just cut the price by $50,000, causing it to hit my feed, so we jumped on it. The home had been handed over to Charleston County, so it had a padlock on the door; within a few minutes of our first visit, the cops showed up to see our Realtor's ID; they had surveillance on the home, given its history. I remember our agent's disgust as she assured us this was not the house for us, about the same time that Katie started crying, confident that I would think it was the one.

I was never distracted by the smell of the house, knowing the work that needed to be done would replace the funk with freshness. I stepped over the holes in the floor, knowing we'd have new flooring. In the few minutes that Katie and our agent had spent with their faces covered, slowly walking around the house, I'd seen every room, climbed into the attic, and inched my way through the crawlspace. This would be our thirteenth move, and while we'd renovated every home we'd ever lived in, we had never done one that large or one that needed that much work.

We closed on the house, and in the following weeks, we had demo parties where we invited friends over to get a workout in by knocking down walls, ripping out cabinets, and gutting everything inside the house. I used almost any available surface to sketch out pictures of what could be. I was energized, it was life-giving, and the future was bright. For me, anyway. Not so much for Katie early on.

Katie couldn't see past the nasty or the scope of renovation to get excited about what could be. She trusted me every step of the way, even when she didn't see it or couldn't feel it. It wasn't until we started putting things back together—painting the walls and installing new flooring to walk on, windows to look out of, and cabinets to use—that the vision became clear to her.

LOOKING FROM WHAT IS TO WHAT COULD BE

Have you ever had to look beyond what is and imagine what could be? Maybe it was a career change after you'd been in a certain line of work for years, but your source of provision, work schedule, family rhythms, and peace of mind, for that matter were firmly rooted in what is. Maybe you stood on a tract of land and tried to imagine what it would look like once the trees were cleared and it was ready for a home to be built. To make a change, you had to look beyond what is and imagine what could be.

We know there is a need for vision, imagination, and faith when establishing things outside of ourselves. But what about having a vision for your marriage? When the need for change, renovation, or building something completely new is inside you. When the walls that need to be torn down can't be seen physically but are felt every day between you and your spouse. Creating that kind of change requires the same vision to imagine what could be.

What is your vision for your marriage? Have you had a conversation about where you are right now? What are you doing? Who are you becoming? Where are you going? And, more importantly, what do you want to be doing, who do you want to be, where do you want to be one year, five years, ten years, twenty-five years from now?

The first step in cultivating or clarifying a vision for your marriage is to turn to the Source of the vision. Do you believe that God has an exciting vision for your marriage? That He wants to bless you and reward you? He's called you to be holy, but do you believe He also wants you to be happy? Do you believe He has plans in store for you that are greater than you know to ask or imagine? All of which is true.

The good news for each of us, regardless of the seasons or circumstances we may be walking through, is that God loves you *and* your marriage! As you begin crafting a vision, here are a couple of faith-building truths to remind yourself of.

God Can Create Something from Nothing

Several weeks ago at church, Katie and I shared our marriage story. Afterward, a man and a woman came up for prayer with their daughter. The man lived in Massachusetts, and the woman lived in Charleston with their daughter. They'd been divorced for years and had tried dating other people.

The husband had flown down for the weekend to surprise the daughter. None of them had plans for Sunday, so the daughter invited them to church, and it happened to be the weekend when Katie and I were sharing our story. They came up for prayer because they sensed that God was involved; their attendance on this particular Sunday wasn't random. The door had long been closed on their marriage, there was no need for communication, and the relationship status was "nothing"; yet God was doing something.

Genesis 1:1 says, "In the beginning God created the heavens and the earth." Most of the Old Testament was originally written in Hebrew, and the Hebrew word used for "created" is *bara*, which means "to form or shape something from nothing."[1] It is a word used eight times in the first seven verses of the Bible. Before we know anything else about God's heart, nature, or character, we learn that He is the God who can create something from nothing. He can look beyond what is, see what could be, and bring it about.

It is amazing. That's who our God is. And it is what He can do for you! Are you having difficulty coming up with a vision because the best descriptor of your current relationship status is "nothing"? Your thoughts are elsewhere, and your feelings are far gone. Don't worry; He can move in your life, stir your heart, and bring a vision that will blow you away.

God Can Create Beauty from Brokenness

Throughout the Old Testament, God used prophets to communicate with His people. Each prophet came at a different point in history and had different audiences and styles unique to them. However, one thing they had in common was the ability to hear from God and see what He wanted to do in the spiritual realm. Because of that, they were commonly referred to as *seers*. For example, 1 Samuel 9:9 says, "Formerly in Israel, if someone went to inquire of God, they would say, 'Come, let us go to the seer,' because the prophet of today used to be called a seer."

One of these prophets was Isaiah, whose name means "God saves." God used him to bring a word of warning and hope to His people. He proclaimed the goodness of God and spoke prophetically of the goodness of Christ. Isaiah 61 is one of the most significant chapters because that is where he prophesied the coming of Christ and the nature of His ministry. Read through this text slowly and make note of the contrast in experience that Jesus came to create in the lives of God's people.

> The Spirit of the Sovereign LORD is on me,
>   because the LORD has anointed me
>   to proclaim good news to the poor.
> He has sent me to bind up the brokenhearted,
>   to proclaim freedom for the captives
>   and release from darkness for the prisoners,
> to proclaim the year of the LORD's favor
>   and the day of vengeance of our God,
> to comfort all who mourn,
>   and provide for those who grieve in Zion—
> to bestow on them a crown of beauty
>   instead of ashes,

the oil of joy

    instead of mourning,

and a garment of praise

    instead of a spirit of despair.

They will be called oaks of righteousness,

    a planting of the LORD

    for the display of his splendor. (vv. 1–3)

Good news to the poor, healing for the brokenhearted, freedom for the captives, comfort to those who mourn, provision for those who grieve, beauty instead of ashes, joy instead of mourning—over and over we hear Isaiah prophesy that our coming Savior is the God who creates beautiful things from what is broken. He is the God who brings life to dead places. If you have made a decision to follow Jesus, you embraced the promise that "if anyone is in Christ, he is a new creation. The old has passed away; behold, the new has come" (2 Cor. 5:17 ESV).

He didn't come to make bad people good or good people better; He came to give us new life. And the same power that saves us can also bring new life to your marriage.

It's not surprising these days to hear someone close to you is separating or getting a divorce; it's a pattern of this world. Left to our own sins, desires, and pursuits, it's an all too likely outcome to marriage today. But as believers, we are told, "Do not conform to the pattern of this world, but be transformed by the renewing of your mind" (Rom. 12:2). If your marriage feels dead and done, if the flirt and fun has long passed, turn away from the patterns of this world and to the Source of vision!

PLAN A VISION RETREAT

For more than twenty years of marriage, I've struggled to have a vision for our lives. There have been plenty of times when I've had a vision, but it was usually about a project, renovation, or possession—something to fix, build, change, acquire, or do. All of these were fairly short-term goals that I methodically planned to complete in the next month, six months, two years, and so on. But God has been challenging me to ask myself this question: What compelling vision, God-honoring desire, and dream in my heart am I willing to pursue no matter what?

God invites us as believers to have vision, to set the course and run after it. Habakkuk 2:2 says, "Write the vision and make it plain on tablets, that he may run who reads it" (NKJV). In fact, Proverbs 29:18 warns us of living lives as a people with no vision: "Where there is no vision, the people are unrestrained" (NASB). The purpose of writing the vision, of making it plain, is to stress clarity. Where are you going? What are you going after? We are all going after something in life; it's a question of what. Is it something I want? Or is it something God wants for me? If we will get a vision for His will, His desire, His purpose for our lives, we'll experience the second part of Proverbs 29:18, "But happy is one who keeps the Law" (NASB). Once the vision is clear, the writer in Habakkuk 2:2 then spoke to pace. You can run fast or slow, but running in general denotes a change in pace, an intention to get somewhere quicker than you would have otherwise.

There is a sense of urgency about being clear about and going after God's vision for our lives. We have only one shot.

Having long-term vision for our lives has been much more natural for Katie over the years. I can get locked in on the vision at hand, while Katie is constantly asking who we are becoming, why we are making the decisions we are, whether we'll be the kind of parents our kids want to come home to visit, and so on. Is cultivating long-term vision more natural for one of you than it is the other? Let that be a source of encouragement for you, not a place of division. I love it when Katie asks the big-vision questions because she helps keep the burdens or blessings of today from distracting me from what God is calling us to.

In 2013, Katie and I had our first vision retreat. We booked a room for two nights in downtown Charleston, got a sitter for the kids, and made a loose schedule for our time together. I knew we needed a solid mix of work and play, because the thought of spending the entire time processing questions about our future would not be a life-giving experience for either of us. So we mapped out a schedule for our time together, which we usually do not do for a weekend getaway, but a vision retreat is different. It is setting aside time to have conversations about where you are, where you would like to be, and what life will look like when you get there.

As much as you'd like the conversation to be focused entirely on the future, there is a good chance one of you is a dreamer gifted at envisioning a brighter and better future (Katie) and the other is a realist who knows where you are today in addition to the habits, decisions, and limitations that got you there (me). Additionally, because I tend to talk about *how* when she dreams of *what*, we give each other permission to keep the other focused on the question, not how we'll make it happen. If you are both dreamers, it will be essential to bring clarity to the vision and identify next steps before heading home. If you are both realists, you'll have to push yourself to imagine what could be if time and money were no object and anything were possible.

We built the schedule so we both had something to look forward to. There was something she wanted both days (a run), something I wanted both days (sex), and something we'd enjoy together (shopping) so that mentally we knew pleasure was coming amid the work. While at dinner or walking around shopping, we weren't taking notes or working through questions, though we were free to discuss what we'd worked through or thoughts that came to mind.

Here are a few commitments you can make to your spouse to make the most of your time together:

I will be positive.

Whether it's a Saturday, a weekend getaway, or a series of date nights, invest in finding a place and space to dream about your future. The goal is to clarify who God's called you to be and what He's called you to do. Don't get critical and don't be offended—you are a team! Commit to keeping each other positive ahead of time so that your conversation or time together doesn't get derailed.

I will be present.

Katie and I tend to carry our work with us into evenings and weekends. In part, that is the nature of ministry. We encourage and help each other process solutions to challenges. But a vision retreat is not the time for that.

Have you ever gone camping or stayed in a cabin that you knew ahead of time would have little to no phone reception? Before you left, you let certain people know where you'd be and prepared in such a way to really be free. Treat this retreat like that. Do everything within your power to draw a line in the sand—a time when the retreat begins and ends, where the conversation is focused on "us."

I will be future-focused.

In your thinking, planning, and talking, prioritize what could be over what is. Don't allow the limitations you experience today to determine the parameters of your tomorrow. We know our capacity to change, the degree of satisfaction we experienced, and the provision we've earned only up to this point. What if God has more? What if this retreat and the vision you craft together is what God uses to take your marriage to the next level and ensure you step into the life you've always wanted? We're believing it will!

I will have fun.

Don't take yourself too seriously. This isn't a presentation for the board or a mortgage application where you need all of your documents in order. You are getting away with your person to dream and get clarity on the future you want to build together. Dance, laugh, and be silly. Do things that make you smile while talking about and working on something that will one day make you happy.

If you're seeing this as work and feel any resistance, check yourself. You're not missing out on anything; you're setting the stage for everything. This is going to be amazing.

A NEW FRAME OF MIND

Have you ever noticed how changing a frame transforms the appearance of a picture? The size and color of the frame can demand attention or cause the presence of the frame to go unnoticed. The frame helps establish priority and presentation. The same principle applies to your frame of mind. Now that you've established some parameters as to the conversation's tone and committed to each other that you will own them individually, it is important to have the right frame of mind.

It can be difficult to jump into vision for the future when you just pulled out of the driveway and still feel like you're in the thick of it with work, life, and family. The following questions aim to get your mind in a different place—to prime the pump, if you will. To shake off the tension of today and disappointments of yesterday so that you can imagine a new tomorrow. Each of these questions is made up of multiple questions; don't rush through them. Allow yourselves to reminisce, process, tell stories, and ask even more questions.

1. What did we envision life looking like as we approached marriage? What were the dreams in our hearts? Does our life today in any way resemble the vision we had in the beginning?

2. Tube or motorboat? If we had to pick one that best describes our experience navigating life now, which one are we on? Do we feel like we are slowly drifting and will see what's to come, or are we aggressively pursuing the things we feel called to?

3. How do we each feel about our lives and marriage today? Are we true to who we want to be and what we want to do? Remember, "I will be positive!"

4. If time or money were not an issue and anything were possible, what would we do? Where would we live? How would we use our time? What would we be doing? How would it feel? What kind of impact would it make?

5. What kind of marriage do we have? What kind of marriage do we want? Is who we are today a result of the vision we had and pursued or a result of decisions we made in response to what life brought our way?

6. Imagine we are at the end of our lives. How old are we? What are we doing? Back to present, are there any older couples in our life that embody who we want to become? Why did they come to mind? What is it about them we admire?

7. Any significant takeaways? Has either of us said anything that stands out? Something important to keep in mind that will help shape our vision for the future?

Now that you've had some conversation and given yourselves some time to reflect, evaluate, and imagine, it's time to start working on your vision. At the end of this book you will find an appendix that will help you craft your own vision.

I dare you to take this seriously. Charlie "Tremendous" Jones passed away in 2008; he served as a leader in the personal and professional development industry. His book *Life Is Tremendous* sold millions of copies in multiple languages and is still available for purchase. Other than responding to everyone about any positive movement in their lives with, "Tremendous!" (which is where he picked up his nickname), he's also known for saying, "One of the greatest thoughts I've ever heard is, 'You will be the same in five years as you are today except for the people you meet and the books you read.'"[2] We would add that pursuing a great vision will have great impact on you individually and as a couple. A lack of vision is the single greatest contributing factor that nearly ruined our marriage. Who were we becoming? Where were we going? We were busy experiencing life, not building one. A compelling vision statement will ensure you aren't drifting through life and marriage hoping things work out, but rather working together to build something you'll be proud of.

CONCLUSION

My (Josh) dad was the world's best grandpa. He loved unconditionally, was wildly generous, and freely gave of the most precious resource he had—time. He would sit beside our kids' beds and hold their hands until they fell asleep. Play with them and their toys, entering imaginary worlds. Drive from Columbia to Charleston to surprise them with ice cream after school. Visit theme parks and spend the day creating memories.

He was also known to surprise the kids with gifts. One

of which I couldn't remember the name, so I spent an hour surfing the internet while writing this chapter to discover what it was called: a purple Boohbah Dance Along Zumbah. Yes, that is a real thing. Upon squeezing its hand, it says, "Pipaaa," or so it sounds. One of our girls saw it in a store one day and, of course, he was willing to make the purchase. They would squeeze Boohbah's hand and dance along with it, saying, "Pipa." It was only a matter of time before "Pipa" became "PiPaw," which is how my dad's grandparent name came about. It was sweet because the kids coined it, and he was so smitten with each of them that he didn't care what they called him.

Seeing the progression of his name come about reinforced the reality of who my dad was. My dad chose to live the kind of stories people would one day want to tell of him. He is, without question, the greatest man I've ever known. What he left to chance, however, is the name his grandkids called him.

It was about that time that Katie and I started asking each other, "What do we want our grandkids to call us?" It seems like a crazy question when your kids are three or four years old. We knew we had plenty of time, but the sooner we named those people, the sooner we could envision what their lives would look like. How they'd spend their time. Where they'd live. How they would support their kids and grandkids. How much money they'd need monthly.

We talked about possible names for a long time before we finally landed on Bear and Ruby. We grabbed the Instagram handle and the website associated with our grandparent names, which will one day be a digital photo book of time spent together, experiences shared, and moments made with our tribe. The most significant being Bear and Ruby Camp. We have seven kids, and while we have no expectation or clue as to how many kids each will have, the dinner table conversation around how many kids they want and what their names will be is usually between three and five. So if we go with four, we will likely end up with twenty-five to thirty grandkids! We have plans to travel to wherever they may live to spend a week with them, meeting their friends and experiencing their world. But one week of every summer, all the cousins will come to us so that mom and dad can plan an epic vacation. It will be every grandkid's favorite week of the summer. They'll never forget the swag, games, late nights, good food, and adventures.

I'm not exactly sure how we landed on Bear and Ruby, but once we did, we fully committed. On our thirteenth wedding anniversary, Katie declared it to be "the year of the tattoo." She wanted her name somewhere on my body; after brainstorming what and where, we landed on something that satisfied Katie's wishes and was in line with our vision for the future. We'd seen people get their wedding band tattooed on their ring fingers; we opted to get our grandparent names on them. I got Ruby on my ring finger, and she got Bear on hers.

Once we had grandparent names, we started to envision what their lives looked like and took some steps to invest in them becoming a reality. It opened the door for conversations and a vision that was much more important. We are going to be together—that is the vision. The bigger question that connects our desired future with our present-day lives is, Are we the kind of parents our kids will want to come home to?

I've had many good moments, but I knew the answer was no the first time Katie asked me that question. I'm impatient and hardworking with a zero-tolerance policy for half-hearted work. Stewardship is a big priority for me—how you steward what you've been given and the opportunities you have will largely influence those God entrusts you with in the future. I tend to lose my mind when beds aren't made, toys are broken, or stuff is left out.

Katie, on the other hand, doesn't care about stuff. She's much more mindful of who the children are becoming. Their tone with their siblings and the kind of friends they are. Are they thoughtful? Compassionate? She's constantly watching and praying into character attributes. As you can imagine, between the two of us, that can be a lot of correction (and frustration if we aren't careful).

Having a vision has led us to question the path, to ensure the vision becomes a reality. If we aren't fun-loving, moment-making parents, it's unlikely that we will wake up one day and flip a switch to become them. To ensure Bear and Ruby Camp becomes a reality, it can't be a big decision we make later in life; it has to be a thousand small decisions between now and then to ensure we've developed intimate, solid relationships and cultivated every bit of the fruit of the Spirit God allows us to experience. Part of seeing this vision come to pass is due to the kindness, faithfulness, and power of God; our part is solely in the commitment to S.T.A.Y. God knows we'll need plenty of love, joy, peace, patience, kindness, goodness, faithfulness, gentleness, and self-control for a weeklong sleepover with thirty kids.

Whether you know it or not, you are on the road to becoming. Every day, every decision leads you somewhere and shapes you into the person and the couple you will one day be. It's a lot easier to envision that day and ask yourself now, "Do I like him/her? Would I want to spend time around them?" and make the needed changes than it is to continue walking this road and hope it works out. You may be disappointed one day.

I have always been a future girl. My mom used to call me "the hurried child" since I was always looking ahead to the next season. When it comes to vision, these strengths have served me well; however, I struggled when it came to endurance and staying power in marriage. When Josh and I walked through our most profound seasons of pain years ago, I remember thinking and dreaming about the future. I would go to sleep talking to God and say, "Well, God, I'll obey You. I'll stay in my marriage, and at the end, I'm sure I have a friend, a pal in Josh. I will learn to get over myself and my passions and desires." I look back on these half-hearted prayers and realize how little that girl knew about our great God. Wow, how I underestimated Him!

The same God who created, authored, and began the spark of love in two random strangers would grow that spark into a safe and lasting oak tree. That firm and rooted tree of love would go on to hold emotion and passion that I could not even fathom back then. If you had told me that Josh would be my favorite person in the world, continue to give me butterflies when he glanced in my direction at a party, make me giggle as we laughed across the table at our inside jokes, and still make me weak in the knees, I never would have believed you.

God authors our emotions, and the truth about endurance is that your marriage was made to sustain you through the hard times. The covenant and vows you made to each other and to God were crafted to help you endure the time when sexy seems to be lost. All couples will move in and out of seasons of ease in marriage, and some couples will walk through lows that most of us cannot imagine. However, the hope we have comes only from God. He took me and Josh from a place of misery to ministry, so we know that He can restore your fountains of emotions so they once again flow with passion and desire.

God can renew the trust and safety you once felt so strongly, no matter what you've gone through or are facing today. He can create a marriage in which you are the most passionate of lovers, the closest of friends, and the biggest encouragers. Will you let hope rise in you? He wants to set your marriage as a city on a hill to share His great love story. All you have to do is what can feel like the most challenging thing: S.T.A.Y.

APPENDIX

CREATE YOUR
SHARED VISION

*B*efore being married, you were free to dream. Anything was possible. Not really, but there were times when it felt that way. You weren't nearly as aware of how challenging life could be, the frustration you'd experience due to your finances, how everything would change when kids came along, or how difficult it is to balance the responsibilities of work and life. Stress has a way of stifling dreams and killing vision.

God has brought you two together for a reason, and having a shared vision for your marriage will help ensure you discover why. Before you cultivate a lifelong vision, let's look at the next five to ten years. Where do you see yourselves? What is the vision? Let's get started!

1. WHAT ARE OUR CORE VALUES?

If you're not sure, think about it this way: How do people describe you? Generous? Hardworking? Joyful? Encouraging? Having clarity on your core values will help ensure you build a future that is meaningful. Your values are a reflection of what you believe and are made visible by your behaviors. Generous people are known to give, encouraging people are known for their kind words, and so on. Identifying your unique values will help you be true to who God made you to be and ensure you are proud of the future you build together.

2. WHAT PROBLEM MUST BE SOLVED, NEED MET, OR CHANGE MADE?

What was the first thing that came to mind? It could be something as big as hunger or poverty in a third world country, as close as a foster care crisis in your community, or as personal as your work schedule. Identifying what's bothering you can be a primary source of inspiration for both short- and long-term vision. As you think through this question, start a list. Upon completion, prioritize them based on order of importance.

3. WHO ARE WE HELPING
BY ACCOMPLISHING
QUESTION NUMBER 2?

Is there a unique nationality, demographic, gender, or age group that we are serving? Knowing you are burdened for widows, the homeless, teenagers, or the Togolese people will help you identify some of your next steps.

4. WHAT ONE THING DO
WE NEED TO DO NOW?

What makes you always say, "We should do that!"? Something that you've said, "One day . . ." about long enough? Maybe you tried before and failed, so you threw in the towel. Maybe you've never tried at all.

With your spouse, fill in the blank to this sentence: We *have* to _____ (write a book, start a business, go on a mission trip, have a baby, or give away a million dollars). However you complete that sentence, conviction is a good indicator of calling. When you have a degree of certainty behind something you "have to do," it's important to ask why. It's also important to ask when; now may be the time to make it a priority.

5. WHERE DO WE SEE OURSELVES
IN THE NEXT TEN YEARS?

How old will we be? What's our marriage like? How old will our kids be? Do we have grandkids? What major life milestones will we experience? How will God use us?

6. HAVE FUTURE-YOU ANSWER,
"WHAT HAPPENED THESE
PAST TEN YEARS?"

Review your answers to question 5. Highlight words or phrases that stand out and use them to answer this question: What happened?

7. CHANGE YOUR RESPONSES TO QUESTION 6 AND MAKE IT PRESENT OR FUTURE TENSE.

Keep it simple, and use "we" statements. Remember, this is your vision statement; it can capture some of your personality, can include a lyric from your favorite song, Bible verse, or inside joke. A vision statement's power is in its ability to bring about clarity and move you toward a compelling future.

It's okay to pursue what may seem impossible or continue to entertain a vision that seems beyond our reach. Aren't you tired of settling for what is realistic and easily attainable? Instead of asking what-if questions, too often we get bogged down in "I have to" statements, which can leave us feeling like we are getting by instead of pursuing a shared vision. That said, "I am certain that God, who began the good work within you, will continue his work until it is finally finished on the day when Christ Jesus returns" (Phil. 1:6 NLT).

ACKNOWLEDGMENTS

*I*n our darkest season it was the voice of Jesus that gave us assurance we could rebuild our marriage steadfast in His love. It started there with His words about marriage, His voice of love, His miracle-working power that can truly bring dead things to life. But it did not end there. Without the following voices this story would not have made its way to principles that could be multiplied, much less pages. We are grateful to Him for being the hero. We are thankful for the following voices that, even once realizing we were the Anti-Hero (thank you, T Swift!), made us believe He could use this mess to bring healing to others.

Pastor Don Brock of Gateway Church

Several years before our marriage crisis, I interviewed for a position with Don Brock at Gateway Baptist Church. While

I loved Don, I felt like we were supposed to pursue an opportunity at another church. Don didn't treat me like just another applicant. He checked in every few months. We'd grab lunch, he'd call to let me know he was proud of me, thinking about me, and praying for us. Even with a family, staff, and large congregation of his own, he chose to pursue, care for, and encourage me. When things got ugly, he doubled down. He started calling daily, offering counsel and actively fighting for our marriage. Don was a spiritual father to me in our darkest days. Like many of you, he had not experienced what we were walking through. But he faithfully practiced the ministry of presence by showing up, reaching out, and letting me piggyback on his faith. His servant-hearted sacrifice makes me emotional to this day. In the ugliest moments when others seemed to step out, he stepped in and embodied the heart of God.

Mac and Cindy Lake

Upon moving to Charleston, we joined a married couples small group with Mac and Cindy Lake. Katie's mom, Debbie Hopper, had told me about Mac for years. He was a pastor at Seacoast Church at the time, and Debbie would often pass along his messages or leadership principles he had shared for encouragement. Before moving to Charleston I'd drive up from Columbia to meet with Mac occasionally. I'd come away from time with him desiring to be like him as a husband, father, and pastor. He gave me a vision of the kind of man I wanted to be. Within five to six weeks of joining their group, every other couple had to back out because of transfers, shift changes, kids' sports schedules, among other things, until it was only Mac, Cindy, Katie, and I every Friday night from 6:00 to 10:00 p.m. We'd show up early and leave late. Mac and Cindy created a safe space for us. It got to where we wouldn't touch anything overly controversial Saturday to Thursday, knowing we could bring it up with Mac and Cindy on Friday. Having never experienced what we were walking through, they made themselves available to listen, encourage, and love the two of us. I remember moments where Cindy would hold Katie's face while reminding her of who she was in Christ and what He was capable of doing in our marriage. They faithfully practiced the ministry of presence by showing up, reaching out, and letting us piggyback on their faith. Their servant-hearted sacrifice makes us emotional to this day. In the ugliest moments when others seemed to step out, they stepped in and embodied the heart of God.

Pastors Greg and Debbie Surratt, Josh and Lisa Surratt of Seacoast Church

Thank you for providing a church for the broken. Thanks for allowing us to heal and be restored in marriage and in ministry under your leadership. The lessons you all teach with your lives about the Father's heart have impacted thousands, and our family is one of them. We will never be the same after encountering God's love through the church family called Seacoast.

Trinity McFadden of The Bindery Agency

Thank you for taking a risk on us, fighting for us, and believing in this message. You have been a gift to us and a confirmation of God's leading and direction for each step of this journey!

W Publishing Team

Kyle Olund, you took a risk on first-time authors with a passion to see marriages renewed. You have made our first book a true joy and gift in our lives. We are eternally grateful that you will get this message into the hands of those who need it.

Liz Morrow

To the ones who do all the Zoom calls to help you birth a dream. We can't recommend a book proposal magician enough. Thank you for sifting out the hours of conversation, tears, and hope and presenting a document others could embrace.

Justin Jaquith

Thank you for taking our story and practically working steps and principles easy to access and take hold of. You do it for an audience of one; we are so grateful.

To our family who has supported us through this season and every season. Deb and Gibson Hopper for speaking life into us daily, for date night child care in the years it mattered most, and for offering a seat at your table every Sunday. Wayne and Libby Walters for leading the way in generosity, grace, and encouragement. You have served and supported us since Katie ran over the mailbox. We miss you, PiPaw. Jess Connolly, for leading the way. Don't think we'd have a family of authors if it weren't for you. Cheers to five authors and four books being released in 2024! We are just getting started!

To the A-Team! Our children: AnnaJaye, Abigail, Abel, Asher, Ari, Anthem, and Adele. You have always been our dream. What the Enemy meant to stop will lead to a legacy of generations that find their souls' rest in our Lord. You love us when we are broken, unlovable, and disobedient, and we love you back. Always.

NOTES

Chapter 2: "Father, Forgive Them"

1. Jessica Saggio, "Major Key Alert: Why Everyone Is Obsessed with DJ Khaled," *Florida Today*, February 25, 2016, https://www.floridatoday.com/story/life/family/2016/02/25/major-key-alert-why-everyone-obsessed-dj-khaled/80934828/.

2. "5547. Christos," Bible Hub, *Strong's Concordance*, accessed October 1, 2023, https://biblehub.com/greek/5547.htm; "3323. Messias," Bible Hub, *Strong's Concordance*, accessed October 1, 2023, https://biblehub.com/greek/3323.htm.

Chapter 3: Worship Is Warfare

1. Sinach, vocalist, "Way Maker," written by Sinach, audio producer Mayo, December 31, 2015, https://youtu.be/n4XWfwLHeLM.

2. Alan Fogel, "Emotional and Physical Pain Activate Similar Brain Regions," *Psychology Today*, April 19, 2012, https://

189

www.psychologytoday.com/us/blog/body-sense/201204
/emotional-and-physical-pain-activate-similar-brain-regions.

3. Blue Letter Bible, s.v. *ochuromu*, blueletterbible.com for Greek
and Hebrew words, accessed September 2, 2023.

Chapter 5: When My Heart Feels Far Away

1. Katie Wedell, Lucille Sherman, and Sky Chadde, "Midwest
Farmers Face a Crisis. Hundreds Are Dying by Suicide," *USA
Today*, March 9, 2020, https://www.usatoday.com/in-depth
/news/investigations/2020/03/09/climate-tariffs-debt-and
-isolation-drive-some-farmers-suicide/4955865002/.

2. Wedell, Sherman, and Chadde, "Midwest Farmers Face a
Crisis."

Chapter 6: An Invitation to a Newer, Deeper Love

1. This quote, with slight variation in wording, is attributed to
both Tony Robbins and Henry Cloud.

Chapter 8: Winning with Community

1. Jamie Ballard, "Most 'Complete Extroverts' Say Their
Partners Are Extroverts Too; Introverts Are More Split,"
YouGov, July 16, 2021, https://today.yougov.com/topics
/society/articles-reports/2021/07/16/extroverts-introverts
-dating-poll-data.

2. Craig Groeschel, "Best Way to Avoid an Overwhelming
Life," sermon at Life.Church, July 10, 2022, https://youtu.be
/hWAGVKkKlmo.

Chapter 11: Just Around the Corner

1. Blue Letter Bible, blueletterbible.com for Greek and Hebrew
words, accessed September 2, 2023.

2. Blue Letter Bible, s.v. *metamorphoo*, blueletterbible.com for
Greek and Hebrew words, accessed September 2, 2023.

3. Blue Letter Bible, blueletterbible.com for Greek and Hebrew words, accessed September 2, 2023.

4. Ferris Jabr, "How Does a Caterpillar Turn into a Butterfly?" *Scientific American*, August 10, 2012, https://www .scientificamerican.com/article/caterpillar-butterfly -metamorphosis-explainer/.

5. Lesley Alderman, "8 Ways to Feel Less Anxious About Things Beyond Your Control," *Washington Post*, September 13, 2022, https://www.washingtonpost.com /wellness/2022/09/13/mental-health-hope-fatigue-coping/.

Chapter 13: Your Best Days Are Ahead

1. Blue Letter Bible, s.v. *bara*, blueletterbible.com for Greek and Hebrew words, accessed September 2, 2023.

2. Charlie Jones, *Life Is Tremendous* (Carol Stream, IL: Tyndale Momentum, 1981), chap. 4, "Leaders Are Readers."

ABOUT THE AUTHORS

Josh and Katie Walters lead a nonprofit called Francis + Benedict, serve on staff at Seacoast Church, and are the parents of seven kids. They both have a master's in counseling, and Josh currently serves as the executive pastor of Seacoast Experience. Josh and Katie have experienced the mercy of God in their marriage and see His hand of faithfulness over every area of their lives. It's their mission to bring hope to the hopeless and see people walk in abundant life. They live in Charleston, South Carolina.

NEW *Marriage,* SAME *Couple* WORKBOOK

DON'T LET YOUR WORST DAYS
BE YOUR LAST DAYS

JOSH + KATIE WALTERS

"The *New Marriage, Same Couple Workbook* will help establish hope in your marriage. And it will show you how to create a brand-new marriage, whether you've been married for a short time, or for decades."

FRANCIS + BENEDICT

Dress Beautifully, Think Globally, Make a Difference

Josh and Katie Walters are the founders of the non-profit Francis and Benedict. This organization exists to empower and equip skilled Togolese seamstresses by providing them with dignified and sustainable income. Together, we are creating generational change in Togo, West Africa.

How can you support this Kingdom-sized mission?

- Shop the beautiful collections, all hand sewn by our seamstresses!

- Learn about our impact initiatives and become a generous giver.

- Share this mission with your friends and family.

- Pray for the F+B team as they work to create generational change in Togo, West Africa.

SHOP HERE